EDUCATION AND THE RISE
OF THE CORPORATE STATE

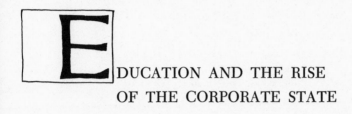

EDUCATION AND THE RISE OF THE CORPORATE STATE

BY JOEL H. SPRING

BEACON PRESS   BOSTON

For Edward A. Krug

CONTENTS

By Ivan Illich

J oel Spring has written a dense and lucid history of progressive liberal politics and the concomitant growth of the American public school system. He has illustrated it carefully with anecdotes, quotations, and statistics, and has orchestrated it around critical summaries of the contributions of more than a dozen men. The fact that he gives equal importance to George W. Perkins, Herbert Croly, Samuel Gompers, and G. R. Taylor alongside William Chandler Bagley, Colin Scott, John Dewey, and Wilson Gill points to the uniqueness of his endeavor. In his perspective the history of schooling turns out to be the account of the increasing sophistication, hypocrisy, and futility of social controls wearing the masks of preparation for democratic participation.

Spring's book is not only important but useful. During the last ten years schools have increasingly lost their pedagogical, their political, and their economic legitimacy. Most contemporary critics of education by school start from this dysfunction of present schools and suggest better schools by which people can be prepared *for* society. They do not question the purpose of institutionalized and compulsory learning.

After following Spring's account, only the ingenue or the

callous will miss his point: the primary purpose of the school system is social control for a corporate state, and for an economy which has as its goal the efficient production and the disciplined consumption of growing amounts of goods and services. Eight decades of pedagogical reform within the school were justified as the means to increase indirect, pervasive, and effective social controls notwithstanding the humanistic freedoms which served as platforms for the reformers.

Unless criticism of educational systems directly questions the possibility of humanistic education through obligatory confinement (even though this confinement be the result of benevolent seduction into "free" schools) the present wave of new educators will only contribute to making the schools more effective in the production of members of a machinelike society. This conclusion appears clearly in the final chapter in which Spring contrasts Fromm and Ellul with McLuhan.

Education and the Rise of the Corporate State could soon become standard reading not just in educational but also in economic, political, and cultural history.

INTRODUCTION

I t was Edward Krug's *The Shaping of the American High School* that first interested me in the meaning of American liberal rhetoric as applied to education. Education, like democracy, is something everyone in America says they support, but exactly what they mean by education is never clearly stated. Liberalism in the twentieth century in both its early Progressive form and later development has staunchly supported education as a cure for social and economic problems. This, of course, had been Horace Mann's dream in the nineteenth century, but its full institutional realization occurred in the early twentieth century. For the past seventy years public educational institutions have played a leading role in campaigns to end urban poverty and crime, Americanize foreigners, heal the wounds of race relations, and rejuvenate an often sagging democratic spirit.

The purpose of this book is to explore the exact meaning Progressives gave to public education during its most formative period at the beginning of the twentieth century. Who were the Progressives is a highly debatable and elusive question. For the purpose of my study I am defining as the main body of Progressives those American leaders who adopted as the image of the good society a highly organized and smoothly working corporate structure. Members of this group of Progressives held a variety of positions in society. They were labor leaders, corporation heads, financiers, politicians, political philosophers, and educators. It is the basic thesis of this study that this image of society played an influential role in shaping the form and direction of American public education in the twentieth century.

The image of the good society as a highly organized corporate structure was the result of city living and large scale industrial organizations. Urban life impressed Americans with the need for efficient and organized government to counter the potential chaos caused by packing millions of people into small areas. The same form of chaos was felt in industrial competition and labor strife. The organizational model which promised a solution to these problems was the large corporation run on the lines of scientific management. Specialization, cooperation, and scientific planning offered a means by which an ever increasingly complex society could organize its institutions.

Education reacted to this image in two major ways. On the one hand education adopted the goal of training the type of man required by this type of organization. This meant teaching the student how to cooperate with others and work in groups. This resulted in class and school programs designed to socialize the student and prepare him for a life of cooperation. On the other hand education was viewed as one institution working with others to assure the progress and efficient operation of the social system. This meant that the schools trained pupils in the specialized skills required by the new corporate organization. Ideally the students would be able to leave school and directly enter a social niche. To a great extent children became a form of natural resource that was to be molded by the schools and fed into the industrial machine. Vocational guidance and the junior high school were two of the important results of this form of thinking.

One reason these changes in education were adopted was because of support by the business community. Education which supplied industry with manpower was good for business and, according to some, what was good for business was good for society. Business supported many of the innovations in education because they promised a healthier and better trained worker. For instance, industrialists supported cooking classes because it was felt the worker would be more contented and efficient if his wife knew how to manage the family money and prepare healthy meals with inexpensive food items. Business also supported social activity programs in the school because they needed and wanted men who would cooperate with fellow workers. Organized industry wanted the organization man.

These changes in education also reflected a definition of individualism which stressed cooperation and self-sacrifice to society. One function of the schools was to assure that something called "selfish individualism" was rooted out. The cooperative man, according to this definition, gained his individualism through a unique contribution to society. This meant performing a specialized role in the social organism. The schools supported something called individualism by training the individual for that specialized place in society. The popular educational phrases of "individualizing instruction," and "meeting individual needs" meant nothing more than educating a child for the role it was determined he would fill in society.

If educational rhetoric was at all representative of Progressive rhetoric, it suggests a pattern of thinking that might have been present in the early stages of twentieth century American liberalism. In this rhetoric the good society meant the efficiently organized society that was producing the maximum amount of goods. Man was viewed as a raw material whose worth was determined by his contribution to the system. Large organizational units and centralized government were accepted as the best forms of social institutions. To paraphrase John F. Kennedy, the attitude became one of what can you do for your country, not what can your country do for you.

The relationship between Progressive politics and the development of the American public school in the twentieth century has largely been neglected. Lawrence Cremin's pioneer book, *The Transformation of the Schools,* dealt with the problem in very general terms without ever specifically relating Progressive ideology to specific changes in the schools. Cremin's broad approach to the topic left untouched important areas of educational change which, incidentally, were to provide the basic structure and goals for American public schools in the twentieth century. One book that does show the relationship between the Progressive concept of the corporation and the administration of the schools is Raymond Callahan's *Education and the Cult of Efficiency.*

More recent interpretations of Progressive politics have stressed the concept of the corporate state. One book with this theme is James Weinstein's *Corporate Ideal in the Liberal State.* While the first chapter of this book was written before the author had knowledge of Weinstein's work, the concepts of the corporate state are strikingly parallel. The major difference, of course, is that this book focuses on education as one of the major social institutions of modern society and is primarily concerned with the nature of its development and future.

I would like to thank the many people who have given me advice and encouragement. Of particular importance was Professor Edward A. Krug of the University of Wisconsin. I had the privilege of being Professor Krug's research assistant for three very profitable and rewarding years. Others who aided me in the initial writing were Merle Borrowman, Dean of the School of Education at the University of California; Clarence Karier, Professor of History of Education at the University of Illinois; and Jurgen Herbst, Professor of Educational Policy Studies at the University of Wisconsin. The librarians at the University of Wisconsin and the Wisconsin State Historical Society provided me with much needed help in locating material. I would also like to thank Ivan Illich for the initial publication of the book as a CIDOC Cuaderno in February of 1971.

EDUCATION AND THE RISE
OF THE CORPORATE STATE

CHAPTER ONE

THE PHILOSOPHY OF THE CORPORATE STATE

The corporate image of society turned American schools into a central social institution for the production of men and women who conformed to the needs and expectations of a corporate and technocratic world. This image of society was shared by the emerging elite in business, labor unions, politics, and education and provided the organizing framework for dealing with the rapid industrialization and urbanization of the United States at the beginning of the twentieth century. The institutions and institutional methods developed during this period established the dominant institutional style for more than the next half of the century.

The image of the corporate society was the product of a subtle interweaving of social and economic forces. On the one hand, the rise of modern technology and rapid urbanization at the beginning of the century dictated the need for a new organizational framework for American life. On the other hand, there were the real problems of urban poverty and disorganization, violent labor strife, economic monopolies, and government corruption which needed to be solved. The corporate state was envisioned as a solution to these problems, not only because it was considered the most viable solution, but also because it supported the interests and actions of the emerging elite in business and labor unions. The public schools of the twentieth century were organized to meet the needs of the corporate state and consequently, to protect the interests of the ruling elite and the technological machine.

The philosophy of the corporate state upon which modern institutions were built was formed during a transitional period in history in the late nineteenth and early twentieth centuries. Americans living in the changing urban and industrial world of this period were convinced that their era was a bridge between a traditional agrarian America of independent yeomen and a future dependent on cooperative activities in large-scale industries and vast urban areas. Early American society was conceived of as a time when growth and progress resulted from everyone working for his own self-interest as an independent economic unit without the restraints of a tightly knit social organization. By the end of the century many Americans believed this conception of society was no longer relevant to the urban and industrial world of the post–Civil War period. Future progress, it was believed, would result from cooperation and not competition. The vision of America as a land of independent yeomen had to be replaced with a corporate image of society where social relationships were to center around large-scale organizations. Within the corporate organization of society each man was to do a specialized task in cooperation with the entire social system. One effect of this changing concept of social organization was the abandonment of a definition of individualism that stressed independence for a definition that included self-sacrifice and cooperation.

In education this changing image of society resulted in stressing the teaching of social cooperation and group work. Michael V. O'Shea, a professor of education at the University of Wisconsin, in 1909 summed up these new objectives of education as bringing the individual "into harmony with the customs, ideals, and institutions of present-day society. Intense individualistic feelings and actions must be brought under control, and cooperation must largely take the place of original tendencies to opposition and aggression."[1] Another principle of corporate organization was specialization accompanying cooperation. In a social context this meant everyone had to have his own job to do for the good of the total social organism. Within factories a product was completed more efficiently if different people concentrated on the different steps of production. Social cooperation became essential for the organization of specialized skills needed to complete any given task. An educator, William Badley, in 1904 called the type of man needed for this corporate process, socially efficient. He described this man as one who performed his specialized productive task for society, interfering "as little as possible with efforts of others . . . sacrificing his own pleasure when this interferes with the productive efforts of his fellows . . . [and] when its gratification will not directly or indirectly lead to social advancement."[2]

The corporate view of society was a result of American reaction to the growth of large urban areas and industrial complexes following the Civil War. The problems of a growing urban society suggested that the style of city life should be cooperative and not competitive. The sevenfold increase in urban population between 1860 and 1910 created chaos in the existing systems of municipal governments. These problems were complicated by the social maladjustment and instability of the groups migrating to urban centers from rural areas in the United States and Europe. In 1910 only 21.6 percent of the 11,826,000 new city dwellers were the result of natural increase. Of the others 41 percent were from abroad, 29.8 percent were native rural-to-urban, and 7.6 percent were in areas newly incorporated into existing cities.[3] The adjustment problems for European immigrants were compounded by the fact that they had previously dwelt mainly in rural areas of Europe.

Native Americans often exhibited an hysterical concern that the economic and social problems of urban civilization were bringing America to the brink of social chaos and class warfare. Many believed, as one writer stated in 1901, that cities could not be made livable and moral if each individual was allowed to assert "what he believes to be his economic interests."[4] This meant that the style of urban living required a cooperative form of existence as opposed to the rugged economic individualism hailed in American mythology. The theme of cooperative individualism proved a double-edged sword when applied to urban problems. It was used both to create a sense of community and to assure economic and political advantages to certain social and economic groups. As will be shown in later chapters, urban reformers used the theme of cooperation to extend their powers over bosses and immigrant groups. This created in urban educational systems the strange phenomenon of decreasing local control of the schools and increasing local use of the schools, both occurring at the same time.

Americans did not easily adjust to the idea that modern urban and industrial civilization required the subordination of the individual to group interests. One classic example of this American dilemma was Ray Stannard Baker, a firebrand magazine writer of the muckraking tradition, who considered the reaching of this conclusion one of the major steps in his life. Baker's career brought him into contact with the major social and economic problems of the era and forced him to redefine his whole concept of the meaning of American life. Baker was haunted throughout his life by the dream of writing the great American novel, a novel, he hoped, that would give the American people an identity and an answer to the problems confronting the period. Baker's personal concern was awakened in 1894 when he followed Coxey's army of victims of the depression from Massillon, Ohio, to the steps of the Capitol building in Washington. The same year brought him into contact with the Pullman strike where he watched federal troops fire not only at strikers but at innocent bystanders, one of whom fell at Baker's feet. He found himself disappointed with the political solutions offered in 1896. After hearing part of William Jennings Bryan's Cross of Gold speech at the Chicago Democratic convention, he followed the presidential candidate to a smoke-filled hotel bridal suite. He watched Bryan standing on the bridal bed give a speech that "went straight into the hearts of his hearers without hurting their heads." In 1900 Baker took a leave of absence from *McClure's* magazine and went West to ponder his own life and the direction of his country's. While riding on the desert he came to a conclusion about life which he wrote was simple but "which I had been so long in reaching, [it] seemed to glow with reality." He concluded, "It is a crowded world. There is no longer, anywhere, any escape for me, or anybody else, from living in it." In 1901 he left the desert and moved into a dark apartment in Los Angeles. Sitting in Los Angeles with the memories of the 1890's haunting him he outlined a never-to-be-completed great American novel. The great American novel was to be two novels. The first, called *The Water-Lord,* was to be a searching presentation of the spirit of the American pioneer. The second novel was to deal with what Baker clearly saw as the major problem facing America, "the Art of Living in a Crowded World." The story of the spirit of the American pioneer was to be set during a period in American history when the vast frontiers allowed indepen-dence and an isolated individualism. The problems of the modern world were to be handled in terms of the closing of the frontier. Baker wrote, "This was to be the greater of the two, and since it would deal with problems not yet clearly under-stood, would involve much new labor."[5]

Fear of social class warfare pervaded the literature of late nineteenth century America and provided a strong motive for urging social cooperation. In New York Jacob Riis warned the American populace in his best selling book, *How the Other Half Lives,* that the slums were splintering American society and creating the "Man with the Knife." "The Man with the Knife" was the title of a very poignant chapter in which Riis tried to show how a man could be brought by poverty to acts of violence. He described a man standing on a street corner watching the rich and affluent of New York rolling down the avenues on their way to spend in an hour of shopping an amount that would have kept his family from want for a whole year. The man driven by the despair of his poverty lunged into the passing crowd and wildly slashed with his knife. Riis wrote that this symbolized what would happen if something was not done about the gap between rich and poor. The man with the knife represented the anarchist who was raising "the danger-cry of which we have lately heard in the shout that never should have been raised on American soil—the shout of the 'masses against the classes'—the solution of violence."[6]

It was in the arena of debate over the issue of competition

versus cooperation with regard to unions and monopolies that the image of the corporate state became clearly defined. Fear of social class warfare, economic conflicts, and the problems of urban living were issues that helped to guide the direction of the debate. The union and monopoly as emerging forms of corporate organizations were considered as either the cause or cure of these problems. One argument was that the concentration of capital and development of labor organizations had disrupted the laissez-faire system causing economic inequalities that could only be cured through antitrust legislation and the restoration of a competitive market. For instance, Senator William E. Borah stated in 1914 in response to the suggestion the problem could be solved through government regulation, "I would never seek to regulate and control monopoly in any form. It is a menace and can no more be controlled than you can regulate and control a cancer in the human system—cut it out root and branch, and do not be afraid to draw blood when you are doing the cutting."[7] The other side of the debate claimed large economic organizations were more efficient and humanitarian because competition was eliminated. This latter argument had the greatest influence on the goals and direction of the public schools.

One of those who helped structure a corporate concept of society was Samuel Gompers, the major leader and dominant influence in the formation of the American Federation of Labor. Gompers' position in the debate over individualistic competition versus a system of large economic units was clearly on the side of the corporate structure. Unions were, after all, working against what they saw to be the destructive forces of competition for employment. Gompers argued throughout his career that unions were just one part of a general organizational revolution taking place in society. During one of his earliest encounters with the new trust system in 1884 when the Chicago packing trust undersold New York meat cutters, Gompers supported the organizational principles of the trust. The corporation, he wrote with regard to the Chicago meat trust, "is a method of group ownership accompanying quantity production which in turn necessitates the dividing of work into operations so that groups performed what was formerly the work of an individual." Gompers argued that the trust only endangered the New York meat cutters "until they learned to protect their individual rights and opportunities through organized activity in groups."[8] Gompers' admiration for trust organization was further revealed when in the early part of the twentieth century he was invited to dine with Charles R. Flint, a man who claimed he organized the first American trust. Gompers reported he told his host that "the trust of centralized control over production was a natural development of industry and legislation to curb this development was really a limitation of the industrial and commercial development of the United States." This statement was made in reference to the Sherman Antitrust Act which threatened both labor and big business. Gompers tried to persuade Flint that unions were like corporations, just "voluntary associations for production and distribution."[9]

According to Gompers the future organization of society was to be along large industrial lines with corporations, organized labor, and organized consumer groups maintaining a check and balance system upon each other. Gompers wrote, "The trust was a phase of the new industrial organization where groups replaced individual effort." The model of society adopted by Gompers clearly replaced the independent economic man of the laissez-faire system with cooperative group effort as the source of progress. Gompers wrote that the problem with corporate growth was finding "the principles and technique for utilizing group action and group production in furtherance of general welfare." He suggested that cooperation of all groups provides the basis for a new social order. The union was to be one organizational contribution to the new corporate society. "The trade union movement," he wrote, "is labor's constructive contribution to democratic regulation of large-scale production. I believe that industry can devise and operate economic principles of administration that will result in constructive control and continuous progress." The democratic control of production would be made possible by the balance between organized labor and business. "So I hold," Gompers stated in full acceptance of the new system, "that trusts should not be suppressed, but regulated and helped to develop constructive control. . . . The corporation form of ownership . . . [has] replaced the system of individual ownership and personal management."[10]

The same type of argument was used by businessmen to explain the organizational revolution. One of the leading spokesmen for the new corporate society and major organizer of Theodore Roosevelt's Progressive party campaign in 1912 was George W. Perkins, a new breed of businessman who viewed the role of business as both an economic and social venture. Perkins justified his work in corporate organization, which included two of the largest industrial combinations, U.S. Steel and International Harvester, by arguing that the fundamental principle of life was cooperation, not competition, and that the modern corporation was one means of achieving a cooperative form of society. This is what he believed in 1902 when he assumed primary responsibility for the House of Morgan in the organization of International Harvester. He brought together the two leading manufacturers of farm implements, the McCormicks and the Deerings, to form a joint corporation which immediately issued preferred stock worth $120,000,000. The formation of International Harvester was designed to reduce competition and give the company control of the market. For Perkins these features were of great social value because the end of competition would lead to more efficient industrial practices and the production of cheaper and better goods.[11]

Perkins' views on the new economic system were not immediately shared by other businessmen. In 1907 when he gave a speech on "The Modern Corporation" at Columbia University he claimed afterwards the president of Columbia, Nicholas Murray Butler, thought of him as a dangerous radical. In his speech he argued economic competition was cruel, wasteful, destructive, and outmoded and that the new corporate form of business represented a social cooperation which was humane and efficient. Perkins also stressed a theme which became quite prevalent in statements supporting the new economic structure. This theme was that the modern corporation was not only good but also necessary and inevitable.

Perkins argued that during former periods men who worked their fields with oxen and crude tools could dispose of their goods through individual trading. With the development of high-speed transportation and communication and new sources of power, more complicated forms of business organization became necessary. The modern corporation was therefore made necessary because of technology.[12] Perkins stressed this theme as he found wider and wider audiences and more and more sympathetic businessmen. It was technology that was forcing men to cooperate. Before the Southern Commercial Congress in Atlanta, Georgia, Perkins stated, "Whether we like it or not, whether it is good for us or not, the great, big, undeniable fact stares us in the face that the inventor has moved us by leaps and bounds, to the 'get-together' age."[13]

Perkins believed one problem with the modern corporation was that it allowed for unscrupulous business activity on a large scale. The solution he offered was government regulation of business. Before the Southern Commercial Congress in 1911 he proposed a business court in Washington to "which our great business problems could go for final adjustment when they could not be settled otherwise." Perkins told the gathered businessmen that their only alternatives to regulation were socialism or government ownership. Under federal regulation Perkins envisioned a progressive society in which prosperity and social justice would be the result of cooperation and not competition. The future social organization, he stated, "would seem to lie through the medium of co-operation, with federal supervision. By co-operation I mean a system of doing business by which all parties interested will enjoy the benefits of the business."[14]

The major organizational platform for this new business philosophy was the National Civic Federation. Both Gompers and Perkins were members of the organization. In fact, Perkins impressed Gompers with "a broad understanding of the problems of industrial relationships."[15] The social composition of the National Civic Federation reflected to a great extent how the new corporate philosophy became the view of the economic elite. One study of the organization found that of the 367 corporations having capital of over $10,000,000, one-third of them were represented. The majority of their representation in the Federation was by presidents and board chairmen. Of the sixty-seven railroads with capital over $10,000,000, sixteen had membership in the Federation. In terms of unions literally all the major union presidents were members including Samuel Gompers and John Mitchell of the United Mine Workers.[16] Gompers' membership caused quite a few heated debates within the American Federation of Labor. Many union members, particularly the socialists, argued he was abandoning the true interests of the worker.[17]

The history of the organization reflected the general trend of business thinking during the early part of the century. Founded in 1900 its original purpose was to provide a common meeting ground for business and labor. It was hoped that through conversation serious labor disputes could be avoided. In 1904 the organization shifted gears slightly and began concentrating upon employee welfare programs. This involved business and labor leaders in discussions over methods of humanizing the industrial process. By 1908 the atmosphere had changed and the major problem became government intervention in social and economic life. Both labor and business viewed this as a common problem since both were affected by antitrust laws.[18]

What became the general philosophy of the National Civic Federation, as the president of the organization stated in 1908, was that labor "organizes for the same reason that capital does and for no other; and both organize because without organization, neither can enjoy the benefits that come from combined action."[19] The general consensus of the organization was for some form of government regulation which would allow for the continued existence of the new corporate structures. This philosophy, of course, reflected the interests of the member organizations. The new corporate world was their world. It was their world almost to the extent that it defined human existence. At times there tended to emerge from discussion of corporate organizations a sense that what a man was depended upon the type of organization to which he belonged. In other words, corporate identity and individual identity were becoming inseparable. John Mitchell, president of the United Mine Workers, gave the usual economic argument before the organization when he stated, "The organization of labor and the combination of capital is the natural and logical sequence of cruel, wasteful, and ruinous competition." But he also included in his speech a statement that was very indicative of the direction in which the general argument was going. Mitchell told the members of the Federation, "The individual employer has merged his interests and his identity in the modern corporation, and the individual workman has merged his interests and his identity in the trade organization."[20]

The major political movement which gave full expression to this corporate view of society was Theodore Roosevelt's Progressive party campaign in 1912. As mentioned previously, George Perkins played a major role in organizing and conducting the campaign. He served as Roosevelt's right-hand man and acted as chairman of the executive committee of the Progressive party. Previous to 1912 there had been contact between the two men. As early as 1901 Roosevelt was sending drafts of speeches and statements on the trust question to Perkins for his comments. In 1905, Perkins' biographer stated, "Perkins was able to tell Roosevelt that he thought his latest statement on the trust question 'everlastingly right.'"[21]

Roosevelt early in his career adopted the attitude that the economic problem was not the existence of large trusts and organizations but their use for evil purposes. Roosevelt believed great fortunes were not the result of devious business practices but the natural result of an expanding economy. In his 1902 Presidential address he argued that the role of government in the economy should be that of eradicating "evil." By "evil" Roosevelt meant not large corporate organizations, but those trusts that acted in a "bad" manner. Roosevelt told Congress in 1902 that "we can do nothing good in the way of regulating and supervising these corporations until we fix clearly in our minds that we are not attacking the corporations, but endeavoring to do away with any evil in them."[22] It was interesting that the two trusts Roosevelt believed were "good" were the two organized by Perkins, United States Steel and International Harvester.

Roosevelt's fame as a trust-buster was largely the result of a few encounters with evil corporations such as the Northern Securities Corporation. In general Roosevelt maintained a policy that a strong government should regulate corporations to assure that they acted in the public interest. In his first message as President in 1901 he advocated the creation of a federal board based on the model of the Interstate Commerce Commission to supervise the large corporations. He stated that these new giants were the result of "natural causes in the business world" and benefited the entire country.[23] In 1910 at Osawatomie, Kansas, in his famous speech for a "New Nationalism," a speech that became a rallying call for the Bull Moose campaign, he clearly stated his belief that the economic system should be highly organized and regulated for the good of the whole society. He told the gathered crowd, "The right to regulate the use of wealth in the public interest is universally admitted. Let us admit also the right to regulate the terms and conditions of labor, which is the chief element of wealth, directly in the interest of the common good."[24]

The issue of cooperation versus competition proved very divisive in 1912 when the Progressive party was organized after Roosevelt lost the Republican nomination for the Presidency. Many Progressives did not share Roosevelt's views on regulation and supported the restoration of competition. The committee on resolutions of the Progressive party included in the platform a plank endorsing and strengthening the Sherman Antitrust Law. The plank read:

> We favor strengthening the Sherman Law by prohibiting agreements to divide territory or limit output; refusing to sell to customers who buy from business rivals; to sell below cost in certain areas while maintaining high prices in other places; using the power of transportation to aid or injure special business concerns; and other unfair trade practices.

When Perkins saw the statement, he immediately objected and with Roosevelt's aid had the committee delete the entire section. The next day when the original section was read by accident before the convention, Perkins sprang to his feet and shouted, "That does not belong in the platform. We cut it out last night." He immediately left the hall. Roosevelt had to have the secretary of the party delete the antitrust section again and issue a corrected statement to the press. This action was not welcomed by those Progressives about whom one Senator warned Roosevelt before the convention. The Senator wrote Roosevelt warning, "Many Progressives contend for a restoration of competition, believing that it would be better for the country and more conducive to industrial progress. . . ."[25]

Roosevelt's general view of a well-working society combined the virility of the frontier with the workings of the modern corporation. He wanted the virtues of rugged individualism to find their place in the modern cooperative society. As our civilization grows older and more complex, he wrote, "It is true that we need new forms of trained ability, and need to develop men whose lives are devoted wholly to the pursuit of special objects, it is yet also true that we need a greater and not a less development of the fundamental frontier virtues."[26] Like the conservation of resources, the conservation of virtues was to provide grist for the industrial machine. In the modern world rugged individualism was to be directed toward the "pursuit of special objects" in the industrial machine. Speaking in 1907 in Lansing, Michigan, at the semicentennial celebration of the founding of agricultural colleges, he told his audience, "We of the United States must develop a system under which each individual citizen shall be trained so as to be effective individually as an economic unit, and fit to be organized with his fellows so that they can work efficiently together."[27] The new pioneer was to be the virile worker doing his specialized task in the new corporation.

The man who worked out many of the implications of this corporate philosophy was Herbert Croly. Croly's *The Promise of American Life* was published in 1909 when Roosevelt had just stepped down from the Presidency and had begun taking safaris to Africa. On one trip, it was reported, he took Croly's book along and upon returning immediately invited the author to dinner. The book, Roosevelt announced, was "the most profound and illuminating study of our national conditions which has appeared for many years."[28] The reason for the favorable impression upon Roosevelt was that it organized into one total philosophy all of the basic ideas inherent in the reform movements Roosevelt had supported. It brought together all the implications of the corporate revolution taking place in society. Roosevelt felt such a close agreement with Croly's ideas that he adopted Croly's phrase, the "New Nationalism," as a rallying call for his Progressive campaign in 1912.

The Promise of American Life was written as an interpretation of the American historical experience and as a book of political philosophy intended to provide direction for future developments. In the first part of the book the historical development of the promise of American life was traced from the beginnings of the Republic through the Civil War to what Croly labeled the "Contemporary Situation." In his discussion Croly located two dominant traditions in America's development. One was Jeffersonian or Republican tradition which stressed equal rights and consequently, Croly claimed, had provided the basis of the argument for an open competitive marketplace and a self-centered individualism. The other tradition was the Hamiltonian or Federalist. Croly described this tradition as one that sought to use the power of the central government to protect the liberties of all the people. Hamilton, Croly argued, did not believe that freedom was just a matter of no government interference. The lack of government intervention only created conditions that were destructive to human liberties. On choosing between the two traditions, Croly wrote, "I shall not disguise the fact that, on the whole, my own preferences are on the side of Hamilton rather than of Jefferson."[29] The last part of the book was devoted to a discussion of a new form of Federalism for the United States.

Croly defined the promise of American life as "an improving popular economic condition, guaranteed by democratic political institutions, and resulting in moral and social amelioration."[30] The fulfillment of the promise under the dominant Jeffersonian tradition of the nineteenth century was to be accomplished through a combination of self-interest and the natural goodness of human nature. The fallacy of this open-market place philosophy, Croly argued, was that no pre-established harmony existed between the satisfaction of private needs and the accomplishment of morally and socially desirable goals. In other words, Croly rejected the idea that allowing men to pursue their own self interests would naturally create social and economic improvements for the whole society. The only result of allowing economic freedom was irresponsible individualism. The recent economic problems of American society, Croly felt, were not caused by a concentration of wealth but a sense of individual irresponsibility. The power of concentrated wealth could be used to fulfill the promise of American life. Croly contended that this could only be possible when, "in becoming responsible for the subordination of the individual to the demand of a dominant and constructive national purpose, the American state will in effect be making itself responsible for a morally and socially desirable distribution of wealth."[31]

Fostering a sense of national responsibility, Croly believed, could not be accomplished through a policy of antitrust legislation. This he felt was only a reactionary method designed to restore a competitive economy which would continue to nourish irresponsible individualism. The positive approach was to harness the new powers of the large organizations and direct them toward national goals. The corporations and unions represented the major means of achieving the American promise. Croly argued that to correct the abuses performed by unions and corporations, there should be strict federal, not state, regulation. This regulation would also be a means of assuring the fulfillment of national goals. Croly wrote, "The huge corporations have contributed to American economic efficiency. They constitute an important step in the direction of the better organization of industry and commerce."[32] Croly's acceptance of the corporate form of economic organization went so far that he even stated that if "the smaller competitor of the large corporation is unable to keep his head above water with his own exertions, he should be allowed to drown."³³ The same attitude was exhibited toward labor unions. According to Croly unions reduced unnecessary competition among laborers and provided an organization that could be utilized for national purposes. The only danger with unions, Croly felt, was that they might call a strike which was not in the national interest. It was for this reason that there had to be some form of federal intervention in labor disputes. As with corporations Croly was pleased to see organization replace competition in the labor market.

Croly recognized that the new forms of corporate organization profoundly altered social relationships in American society. The rise of the large organization meant individual specialization and, consequently, a loss of homogeneity in the community. The American community of the early nineteenth century, Croly contended, consisted of Americans who disliked organization and specialization. The early Americans' "whole political, social, and economic outlook embodied a society of energetic, optimistic, and prosperous democrats, united by much the same interests, occupations, and point of view."³⁴ It was Croly's belief that during this period Americans were essentially all-around men. The new industrial machines that grew in America after 1870 had changed this by requiring the specialist and the expert. This condition destroyed the possibility of community based upon common occupations and interests. Croly wrote that "the dominant note of the period from 1870 until the present day has been the gradual disintegration of this early national consistency, brought about by economic forces making for specialization and organization in all practical affairs, for social classification, and finally for greater individual distinction."³⁵

The loss of this early form of American community was not viewed by Croly as being disastrous. Specialized organization in politics, industry, and labor promised efficiency and practical rewards that outweighed any losses. He believed that Americans had to accept the fact that the homogeneity of American life had disappeared, never to be recaptured. What had to be found was some substitute that would reunite Americans into a new form of community. Croly wrote that the only way the community could be restored would be "by means of a democratic social ideal, which shall give consistency to American social life, without entailing any essential sacrifice of desirable individual and class distinctions."[36] The social ideal would be the fulfillment of the promise of American life for all people. This ideal would not only command allegiance from all people, but also the goals of economic organizations could be subordinated to it. The American community based upon individual specializations would be reunited through loyalty to a common purpose.

The theme of loyalty to a common social ideal became the "New Nationalism" of Theodore Roosevelt's political campaign. The new nationalistic fervor was to be a common allegiance to social and economic improvements. The themes of cooperation and unity rested on the assumption that individual satisfaction and worth were achieved through participation in a collective endeavor. What this meant and how it was achieved was not at all times clearly stated. The value of organizational efficiency often overshadowed any concern about individual worth. The problem did bother Croly to the extent that he devoted the last chapter of his book to the relationship between the individual and the national purpose.

Croly argued that American individualism had traditionally depended upon the pursuit of economic gain. This form of economic individualism, he stated, had been destructive of true individualism. A genuine individual was defined as having some special quality and purpose that distingushed him from other members of society. Economic individualism had placed monetary self-interest above these qualities. According to Croly the fostering of true individualism would be possible in a society that allowed each citizen to develop his individual talents and acquire a special purpose. Croly wrote, "A man achieves individual distinction, not by the enterprise and vigor with which he accumulates money, but by the zeal and the skill with which he pursues an exclusive interest—an interest usually, but not necessarily, connected with his means of livelihood."[37] In other words individualism, according to Croly, was to be a product of the specialized task a man performed for the corporately organized society. A man's identity was determined by his role in the collective endeavor.

This definition of individualism fully submerged the individual within the organization. Croly wrote that as the expert became a part of a great industrial machine his "individuality tended to disappear in his work."[38] This tied the individual to organizational goals because meaning was imparted to work only through its relationship to some common purpose. If the specialized task were performed purely for economic rewards, it would not contribute to the development of a sense of individualism. He also believed that this form of individualism would develop a sense of community because no matter how much an individual distinguished himself in a particular occupation, he would not feel that he was being separated from his countrymen. In fact, achievement would create a greater sense of community because the value of the task would be defined in terms of its worth to the collective endeavor. In other words, the more an individual achieved, the more he helped his fellow man. This meant individual specialization had to be wedded to the democratic social ideal. Croly wrote that "the American National Promise demands for its fulfillment something more than efficient and excellent individual instruments. It demands, or will eventually demand, that these individuals shall love and wish to serve their fellow-countrymen. . . ."[39]

To achieve this form of individualism required training in a specialized task and the development of allegiance to the ideal of fulfilling the American promise. Croly felt that this could be accomplished through institutional education and a form of national education. Croly wrote, "An individual's education consists primarily in the discipline which he undergoes to fit him both for fruitful association with his fellows and for his own special work."[40] Preparation for one's special work could be accomplished through formal methods. Learning to associate and cooperate with others was another problem and required more imaginative planning. This required the gaining of a sense of national purpose and an awareness of the value of each task in the collective endeavor. The form of schooling required to achieve this purpose was, according to Croly, a national education. The nation's schooling, he wrote, "consists chiefly in experimental collective action aimed at the realization of the collective purpose."[41] He did not specify the exact nature of the experimentation, but it was to be directed toward the achievement of the national promise. This meant changing social and economic institutions in a search for more efficient forms of organization. Croly stated that these two forms of education, individual and national, should parallel each other. "The individual," Croly wrote, "can do much to aid national education by the single-minded and intelligent realization of his own specific purposes; but all individual successes will have little more than an individual interest unless they frequently contribute to the work of national construction."[42] The formal methods of education would only gain meaning and contribute to a true sense of individualism by directing individual training to national and collective purposes.

Croly's definition of individualism fitted the general expectations of human activity in the corporate world. The acceptance of large organization and cooperation as an ideal required a definition of individualism that combined specialization with unity to common purposes. Individual identity was now to be a product of an occupation directed toward some common social goal. This definition of individuality was not just a product of Croly's abstract thinking. It accurately described what was happening in the cities and factories. Both were becoming dependent upon a style of living that required cooperation and specialization. Nor was Croly's statement on individualism unique. Similar ones were implied in most statements dealing with the organizational revolution. They also became a part of the working vocabulary of the schoolman. The phrase, "meeting the needs of individuals," meant in education the development of the special talents of the student so that he could fit into a specialized niche in society. Fitting in also required training in the ability to work with others.

The Progressive concept of a corporate society was held by an extremely influential social group. One could argue that

Roosevelt, Gompers, Perkins, Croly, and the members of the National Civic Federation represented an American elite. One historian has suggested that this group actually shaped the direction and structure of the federal government. His argument is that in 1912 there was no significant difference between Roosevelt and Woodrow Wilson. Wilson is quoted as having said "that the business of the country has been chiefly promoted in recent years by enterprises organized on a great scale and that the vast majority of the men connected with what we have come to call big business are honest, incorruptible, and patriotic." Wilson was in fact a non-radical, anti-Bryan Democrat, which meant an anti-antitrust Democrat. Corporate leaders quickly discovered after his victory over Roosevelt that he also defined the problem as being "good" and "bad" trusts. Under Wilson's administration the major emphasis of government activity was upon regulation of corporations and not their destruction. Wilson's New Freedom was, one historian stated, "more than anything else, government regulation of banking, industry, and railroads."[43]

Corporate businessmen and union leaders had, of course, a personal interest in the acceptance as ideals of both a highly organized society and government regulation. The concept of a corporate society justified their activities and gave them an important social role. The support of government regulation was the result of a fear of a socialistic revolution or of reactionary destruction and of a desire to assure future existence. It has been argued that even though large organizational groups were forming in American society, competition was, in fact, actually increasing. Government regulation was one way of limiting competition through price controls and regulative standards.[44] Whether this was true or not does not detract from the argument that regulation and rationalization of the economic system, when the alternatives were weighed, worked to the advantage of the new corporate structures.

Corporate Progressivism played a large part in defining popular goals. This was particularly true in public education. It was this form of Progressivism that had the greatest impact on the public schools. A corporate society needed, as Croly stated, specialization and cooperation. Educators believed that the schools could accomplish the goal of specialization by providing an education that would meet the needs of individual students in terms of their future occupations. The result of this thinking was a differentiated curriculum and vocational guidance. The goal of cooperation and a sense of common purpose was to be achieved through social activities. The result was an expanded program of extra-curricular school activities and an emphasis on group work in the classroom. The two major institutions that resulted from these changes were the junior high school and the comprehensive high school.

CHAPTER TWO

FACTORY LIFE AND EDUCATION

he development of modern industrial systems shaped the direction of public schooling in a variety of ways. In the first place, inherent in the modern factory was a problem of social organization which required the employer to take an active interest in the social life and character of his worker. Out of this concern grew industrial education programs and social activities which were designed to fit the worker into the modern industrial organization. These industrial programs for the management of workers became models for the type of activities adopted by the public schools. Company periodicals, clubs, assemblies, and other social activities can be considered precursors and models for the whole range of extra-curricular activities that were to become a part of the modern school. In some cases actual programs, like home economics, were transferred from factory education activities to the public schools. In the second place, the modern factory system made direct demands on the public schools to produce workers with the correct social attitudes and skills.

From the very beginning of industrial development in the United States employers attempted to exert paternalistic control over their workers. During the ante-bellum period the textile mills in Lowell, Massachusetts, provided a model for this form of industrial relationship. Of the eight thousand workers at

Lowell in 1845 seven thousand were women. Most of the unmarried female workers lived in company boarding houses under the strict regulation of company supervisors. When the employees were not at their jobs, their free time was taken up with either company planned self-improvement programs or moral and ethical instruction. Any employee found guilty of immoral conduct, using bad language, disrespect, or exhibiting an improper attitude was promptly dismissed. The combination of work, self-improvement through education, and moral scrutiny created a wedding between the church, the school, and the factory.[1]

. There were several reasons for business paternalism. One hope was that the development of an industrial proletariat and the concentration of a working class in slums, like London, could be avoided. There was a fear that a factory system would create a depraved and shiftless working class similar to that of Europe. Another, and more convincing reason, was that paternalistic control was good business. The worker who avoided the tavern, engaged in healthy after-work activities, and lived a moral, thrifty life was probably more efficient on the job than his more loose-living fellow worker. The very values that a moral education were to inculcate were those required by the industrial system. As has been so often stated, there was a very close relationship between the Protestant ethic and the requirements of capitalism. Thrift, respect for authority, steadiness of habits, hard work, and industry were the ideal characteristics of the factory worker.

After the Civil War business paternalism became widespread. Corporations during this period not only felt the need for a moral worker but also for company spirit and unity. The very size of corporations created an entire set of problems dealing with the flow of information and the ability to coordinate the various aspects of the industrial process. The development of assembly lines dependent upon individual specialization made it necessary for laborers to learn how to work together for the smooth flow of production. Solving the problems of unity in the corporate structure and of cooperation on the assembly line was made difficult by the fact that industrial specialization itself isolated the worker and created a loss of a sense of unity. In other words, the actual methods of production worked against the spirit of cooperation and unity needed for a smoothly running organization. Industrial managers therefore had to solve this problem by searching for methods not related to production. What this involved was the expansion of business paternalism to accomplish off the job what could not be accomplished on the job.

One problem caused by the size of corporations was the loss of contact between management and workers. Businessmen often referred to a former golden age when the boss personally knew all of his workers. During this prior period it was believed that the employer managed his workers more effectively because he could respond to their needs and give them a feeling of belonging. William H. Tolman wrote, "In the old times master and man lived and worked together; there was daily touch. Today all is changed . . . the day has passed when the employer is able to individualize those who work for him; not knowing them by name or even by sight, the personal touch, the point of contact has been lost." Tolman was cofounder with Josiah Strong of the American Institute of Social Service, an organization that became a clearing house for industrial betterment projects. His two books on the topic, published in 1900 and 1909, art compendiums of the employee welfare programs of the period. Tolman believed, as did many businessmen, that "it is not desirable, even if it were possible, to return to the earlier days. But for the successful conduct of the businessman today, a point of contact must be established in some way."[2]

One of the earliest programs to establish contact between company and workers was the suggestion system. The pioneer in this field was John H. Patterson, the founder of the National Cash Register Company. During the post–Civil War period Patterson established a model industrial plant in Dayton, Ohio. The factory was professionally landscaped, had anti-pollution devices, and contained within it a museum and lecture hall. One writer on industrial betterment practices felt that Patterson's enterprise was built on a moral foundation because the cash register replaced the evil temptation of the open till. The same writer quoted Patterson as saying that his motto was "Do good and make money, and do more good with the money so made."[3] Patterson introduced the suggestion system because he felt that since the industrialist could no longer have direct contact with all parts of the industrial process, he had to assure some method for people directly involved in the work to get their ideas to the management. It was reported that Patterson conceived of the idea of a suggestion system when, as a collector on the canal between Toledo and Cincinnati, he experienced the feeling of helplessness and frustration at not being recognized by his bosses. Patterson had wired his employers telling them of the source of oak plants needed to move some boats stranded in mud. It was reported, "The answer came back, 'you attend to your business and we will attend to ours.' Such a reception of a valuable hint raised Mr. Patterson's wrath, and he said to his friends, 'If I ever have an employee, I'll hear his suggestions about what he may, perhaps, know better than I do.' "[4]

Other methods Patterson used to give a sense of personal contact and unity were conventions and factory periodicals. It was claimed that Patterson was the first man to organize a formal convention to bring agents and salesmen together. The purpose, of course, was to provide for a flow of information and contact. This was also the purpose of the factory periodical. Tolman quoted a large industrialist as saying, "Our publications are sent to every member of the selling forces throughout the world, to every employee. . . . We cannot, as we would like to do, have conventions and personal meetings with our selling force every week or two, but our monthly fills the gap . . . and keeps all parts of our great organization in close contact." The National Cash Register Corporation issued its first copy of *N.C.R.* in 1892 and by 1905 had five other publications. Other companies quickly followed the lead of National Cash Register. Other examples were the Sherwin Williams Company's *Chameleon* in 1898, H. J. Heinz's *The 57* in 1899, and the Illinois Steel Company's *The Steel Works Club Library Bulletin* in 1904.[5]

One idea that Tolman claimed he introduced in the United States in 1900 was the social secretary. The function of the social secretary was to maintain constant personal contact with the workers. Through this personal contact the social secretary was to improve the worker's life both on and off of the job. Tolman wrote, "The social secretary does not treat the laborers en masse, but maintains his individuality so that the employee feels that he is part of the directing intelligence and not a mere cog in the wheel." The social secretary's duties included administering the company welfare program, assuring that the "industrial army" was well fed, and checking on the family life of the worker. According to Tolman many companies adopted the social secretary idea but under different names. H. J. Heinz hired two workers around 1902 who functioned as social secretaries. The International Harvester Company in 1903 proposed a general plan that would have located a social secretary at each plant. This plan was later scrapped in favor of a permanent bureau established in the general manager's office in Chicago. Some companies, such as R. H. Macy & Co., hired a nurse to watch after the health and general welfare of the employees. Tolman reported that employers through the country were quite enthusiastic about the social secretary idea. Joseph Bancroft & Sons Company wrote Tolman that they used their social secretary as a representative of the employees. It was the secretary's job to report worker grievances to the management. The firm reported in 1908, "We consider that the lady in question has been most useful and is now practically indispensable as a point of contact between our company and its employees."[6]

Another way of bringing the workers together to give them a sense of belonging and unity was through worker clubs and group activities. E. A. Filene of Filene's department store of Boston reported to the Social Education Congress that the store in 1907 had organized a club and workers' association designed to train the employees for cooperative social service. Filene's firm provided their workers with a welfare manager, a doctor, a dentist, an occulist, and a clubhouse. All of these employee benefit programs were under the control of the workers' association. Management and workers were given equal voting power within the association. It was hoped that the combination of association and club activities would give the workers a sense of unity and teach them cooperation and social service. Filene concluded his remarks before the congress with, "We should teach [the workers] . . . to become efficient in their daily tasks and to keep before them constantly a high ideal of social service. We should help them to realize that, 'when work is for the common weal, then work is worship, work is prayer.'"[7]

Employee associations were a widespread means of providing benefits in case of death, sickness, or accidents. Many of them established company pension programs. Meetings of the associations also provided an opportunity for workers to gather on a social basis. The Westinghouse Electric & Manufacturing Company's Foreman's Association was organized in 1903 for "the object of fostering social gatherings for mutual benefit in forming acquaintance with one another." The association organized meetings, smokers, and held an annual banquet. The Association of Employees of the New York Edison Company held regular monthly meetings which combined entertainment with regular business. The meetings were held in the auditorium of the New York Edison Company. A number of the benefit associations functioned as company unions and were designed to maintain control over the worker. The Cleveland Hardware Company would not hire a man unless he would join their association. Once the individual was hired, the association would investigate his background and could accept or reject his application for membership. Tolman reported, "It very often happens that the men know more about the people hired than the firm themselves; sometimes on inquiry why the man was rejected by the mutual benefit association, it has been found that it has been for such a good reason that the firm did not care to employ him." The employee association was also an efficient way for the employer to check worker absenteeism. The Curtis Mutual Benefit Society of the Curtis Publishing Company would appoint an investigating committee within forty-eight hours after the notification of sickness. This became standard practice in many companies because it reduced absenteeism due to "phony" sickness and provided aid so the worker could return to his job sooner.[8]

Many new corporations had their buildings designed to accommodate the social activities of their workers. One of the most spectacular was the H. J. Heinz factory in Pittsburgh. Entrance to the factory was through a time-keeper's building adorned with beautiful stained glass windows depicting "the humble origin of the great works, the seal of the city and mottoes inculcating energy, thrift and contentment." Within the factory a special dining room for women was decorated with pictures and plants. On top of the building was a roof garden where workers could relax. An auditorium was provided for public meetings, entertainments, and social events for both the workers and the entire community. The Heinz building was constructed so that employees could easily reach the 2,500-seat auditorium during their lunch hour to hear a visiting lecturer. Special accommodations were even provided for the fifty factory horses. The horses were housed in a fire proof structure, were fed by an automatic mechanism which filled troughs at the press of a button, were cleaned by electric brushes, and were provided with foot baths, Russian baths, and a hospital.

Some companies built separate clubhouses to foster social activities among their employees.[9] The Warner Brothers Company of Bridgeport, Connecticut, built a two-story clubhouse in 1887. The building contained a lunch room, a parlor, a reading room, a library, and a 550-seat concert hall. The Eagle and Phoenix Mills of Columbus, Georgia, hired a gymnasium director and a porter to run their clubhouse. When the workers of the Celluloid Company of Newark, New Jersey, organized a club, the company donated $40,000 for the construction of a clubhouse. The basement of the building was equipped with two bowling alleys, two shuffleboards, and two tunnels for rifle practice. The entrance to the building had marble steps with mosaic flooring which had the club name inserted across its width.[10] The first floor contained offices, a cafe, and a large billiard room. The J. B. Stetson Company built at one end of its factory a 2,000-seat auditorium furnished with a grand piano and a parlor organ. Stetson also provided for a Sunday school and church within the factory. The average church attendance was reported at 600.[11] The National Cash Register Company provided not only a lecture hall and a museum but also swimming tanks, tennis courts, and a bicycle repair shop.[12]

Another way companies maintained a spirit of unity was to bring all workers together in some annual festivity. The most popular was the corporate Christmas party. One Christmas festival held by the H. J. Heinz Corporation in 1899 was attended by 1,000 people. Gifts were exchanged and gold watches were given to heads of departments who had been with the company from six to twenty-five years.[13] In many companies athletic associations were organized and men and women would gather on non-work days to play team games. Remington Typewriter Company organized an Annual Field Day which was highlighted by a Maypole dance by its female employees. One of the largest and most organized outings of the period was held by the Men's Welfare League of the National Cash Register Company.

In 1905 the company closed its doors for two weeks and 1,700 employees boarded three special excursion trains of ten cars each to travel to a camp at Port Huron, Michigan. The 1,700 employees spent eight days living together in a tent city and eating together in a big dining tent.[14]

Many of the employee welfare programs were the result of employer fear of industrial struggles and of opposition to unionization. One example was George Pullman who began constructing his model company town south of Chicago in 1880. In 1872 Pullman read and reread a popular novel of the day on industrial turmoil. It was Charles Reade's *Put Yourself in His Place*. The novel is set in an English working community where the owner of the major industry shows little concern for the welfare of his employees, consequently they organize secret societies, bomb factories, and terrorize workers who will not join them. Pullman's reaction to this part of the novel was probably the same one he expressed to Andrew Carnegie after the Haymarket Riot in 1886. He wrote to Carnegie after the riot stating his concern about the survival of the democratic system with the "excesses of our turbulent population."[15] The hero of Reade's novel is a young inventor who applies scientific principle to production, improves working conditions, and ends strife between capital and labor. The inspiration Pullman received from this novel partly contributed to his attempt to create a model community which eventually failed under the pressure of the very labor strife he was trying to end. Stephen Buder writes in his study of the Pullman community that "Pullman frequently told friends that Reade's novel had convinced him that capital and labor must learn to co-operate for their mutual benefit."[16]

One of the major attempts to avoid unionization through a company welfare program was that of the Colorado Fuel and Iron Corporation. This corporation controlled more mining towns than any other company in the West. Its control of the southern Colorado Coal Fields made it a major target of the United Mine Workers. The company's resistance to unionization eventually led to the Ludlow massacre in 1914 when an armed clash between miners and state militia in Ludlow, Colorado, resulted in a tent's catching fire and the burning to death of two women and eleven children who had taken refuge under the wooden floor. At least eight other people were killed on the same day. The enraged miners took control of the coal fields and continued fighting until the arrival of federal troops.[17]

The Colorado Fuel and Iron Corporation had tried to avoid unionization by establishing in 1901 a company sociology department and a weekly magazine called *Camp and Plant*. The purpose of the magazine was to improve the image of the company in the eyes of its employees by describing the welfare work of the sociology department. The sociology department, under the direction of a welfare manager, was responsible for the recreational and educational facilities and the sanitary conditions of the company towns. The sociology department of the company also carried on experiments in social control. One example was their temperance experiments. It was reported that in one year they experimented with four different types of saloons in different towns to determine the most effective way of controlling alcoholic consumption. The four types of saloons were the regulated saloons, the restricted club, the soft-drinks club, and the open reform saloon. The regulated saloon was under the control of one person who was responsible for the decency of the place. The restricted club was an organization controlled by its members. They maintained a monopoly over the camp liquor supply. The soft-drinks club supplied only non-alcoholic drinks while the open reform clubs provided both soft and hard drinks.

The most thoroughly organized part of the welfare program was the school system. The company maintained schools in all of its major mining towns. It also organized a uniform course of study so that children would not be placed at a disadvantage if their families had to move from one company town to another. The school buildings in each town were constructed around the same basic design with provisions made for adequate light and ventilation and folding partitions between rooms to allow for more flexible use. The company provided an industrial and normal school session for teachers during their summer vacations. A circulating reference library and an art collection were also available. It was reported that the kindergarten received special emphasis because "it is recognized that this institution not only takes the child in hand at its most impressionable period, but that it furnishes a center from which radiate influences that affect the whole social betterment situation." [18]

The labor problems of both the Colorado Fuel and Iron Corporation and the Pullman community were in part caused by worker dissatisfaction with the management of employee welfare programs. One of the complaints of the United Mine Workers against the Colorado Company was that freedom of speech was being denied in company towns. This accusation was sustained by Reverend Eugene S. Gaddis who served as superintendent of the sociology department until February 1915. After leaving the company, he complained that company officials had dictated the selection of teachers and had obtained the dismissal of those to whom they objected, even though it meant appointing incompetent teachers.[19]

Employee social activities, clubs, and conventions were all designed to produce a worker who in a later period would be called an organization man. A socialized and cooperative individual was the type needed both on the assembly line and in the management team. These activities also served another goal. Since they extended corporate control over the social life of the worker, they could be used to increase his efficiency.

Efficiency during this period of industrial growth meant several things. On the one hand it referred to the time and motion studies of Frederick W. Taylor. These were designed to show what type of motions and routine would complete a particular job the most efficiently. On the other hand, efficiency referred to the physical condition and the moral and social character of the worker. One objective of the employee welfare movement was to assure that the worker had the right character and was in the best physical state to complete his job efficiently. There was strong resentment by workers and labor unions against the Taylor type of efficiency. For instance, the National Civil Federation, an organization of business and union leaders, dropped the discussion of Taylorism when members of the A.F. of L. raised objections. Of course, business officials within the Civic Federation continued to be enthusiastic. Corporate programs to increase moral and social efficiency were not objected to by union officials except where they resulted in company unions. In fact, many meetings between business and labor in the National Civic Federation were devoted to employee welfare programs.[20]

Both of these definitions of efficiency reflected the view that man was a machine. Taylor was essentially trying to train men to have the precision and timing of an industrial machine. It was also quite easy for businessmen discussing employee welfare benefits to draw parallels between tending a machine and tending a man. The president of Illinois Steel stated in 1889 at the dedication of the company's clubhouse that "while they had been planning and contriving for the improvement of their mechanical forces, they had omitted to provide for the repair of the other great and essential power the flesh and blood of the men."[21] The argument for employee programs was that an improved man for an improved machine would mean more production. The task of the new corporate manager was to maintain unity and physical and social efficiency. Tolman wrote, "Never before in the history of the world has the employer had such colossal opportunities for guiding and uplifting the thousands of men and women . . . they hold within their grasp the possibilities of industrial contentment, social stability and communal welfare. . . ."[22]

Most companies agreed that physical efficiency was increased if a nurse or doctor looked after the worker. The health expert served the function of providing aid for any industrial accident and also making sure that the worker properly treated any ailment. The Waltham Watch Company reported to Tolman that a trained nurse was an important factor in increasing plant efficiency. The company wrote, "It is almost impossible to estimate the ground which has been gained in preventing absences from work, prevention of contagion and infection, especially at times when there is a prevalence of disease or possibly a threatened epidemic." It was also being recognized that physical comfort could be a factor in production. Waltham installed chairs that moved on grooved rails to reduce fatigue caused by the supervision of several machines.[23] Improved sanitary facilities reduced disease and improved worker morale. Many companies began providing large wash rooms and baths. The J. H. Williams Company of Brooklyn provided a trough so that their men could wash out their underclothes and a drying closet with hot water pipes.[24] Many companies hoped that ideas on sanitation and health would spread to the worker's family life so that there would be further prevention of lost working time. Tolman wrote, "The provision of the most improved sanitary and hygienic conditions is the very A B C of industrial betterment; it is not charity or welfare work; it is good business, because it enables the worker to labor under such conditions as will allow him to fulfill to the utmost his part of the wage contract."[25]

Exercise and proper diet were used to maintain physical efficiency. Workers at the National Cash Register Company would stop work for a recess in the middle of the forenoon, open the windows, and devote ten minutes to light gymnastic exercises.[26] More common than on-the-job exercise was the organization of athletic teams and the provision for exercise near the factory. For instance, the Solvay Process Company enclosed a five-acre athletic field and built a running track and baseball field.[26] Provisions for noon lunches were made to assure that the worker was able to buy a healthy meal. One writer on industrial betterment programs claimed that Jane Addams organized the first lunch club for the Western Electric Company in 1893.[27] But whether she did or not, by the turn of the century it had become standard practice for new plants to set aside areas for dining rooms. The Patton Paint Company of Milwaukee constructed an elaborate combination dining room and rest room for the physical comfort of their women employees. Every table was decorated with potted plants and on the other side of a "row of gay Japanese screens" was "the rest room, with its comfortable many-cushioned couches, capacious rocking-chairs, its tables heaped up with the newest magazines, and a stationary washstand with a mirror long enough for a girl to see herself from head to foot."[28]

Company cooking classes were one of the major attempts to influence the dietary habits of the worker's family. A temperance experiment carried on by the sociological department of the Colorado Fuel and Iron Company included cooking instruction. It was believed that if the worker "comes home to a supper of tasteless, indigestible food, served without any attempt at making it inviting, or the table attractive, is there any wonder that he seeks the saloon for a stimulant?"[29] Proper meal planning was important because the worker's wife had to learn how to manage the budget so that meals designed to maximize the worker's energy could be served. The Plymouth Cordage Company provided a cooking school for the children of its employees. The children were allowed to attend after the age of eleven when they were taught good "plain cooking . . . how to make a dinner from cheap cuts of meat, the proper food to buy and the correct combinations to use to build up the tissues of the body and brain."[30] A committee of the National Civic Federation reported that southern mills provided instruction in "the proper preparation and serving of food, how to buy groceries, the desirability of cleanliness in the home. . . ." The report commented that it "goes without saying that a good, wholesome meal will make a more healthful body and that the disappearance of slovenliness from the household will make the fireside an attractive and winning competitor to the saloon when the day's work is over."[31]

The company library was one method used to build character. One day in 1901 the Sherwin Williams Paint Factory sounded its whistle at 4:30 to gather the entire plant staff for the dedication of a new reading clubroom. The company president told the assembled workers, "We have been trying in many ways to help those who were laboring with us to make them more comfortable, more intelligent and happier and better men and women."[32] Five and six thousand volume libraries became standard features of new factories. Some companies even made special arrangements so that it would be easy for their employees to get books. For instance, Pullman provided one library that was very well furnished, and another very austere one for workers coming from work. It was explained that the latter had been thoughtfully provided for those who could not be tempted into the main rooms . . . with soiled hands and faces. . . ."[33] The National Cash Register Company provided a library with rolling shelves that traveled from department to department. Workers could return books and place orders for others when the library was wheeled into their work area. In 1899 the Seaboard Air Line Railroad reorganized its library into a free traveling library which eventually circulated 6,000 volumes to the small towns and villages along its route. In 1904 the Southern Pacific Railroad organized a free traveling library for its section gangs. It eventually included other people within the area of the section gangs in its circulation. For the Southern Pacific the library served as both a method of industrial improvement and as a public relations technique. One general passenger agent wrote Tolman in 1907, "We find that the

library has caused the public generally along our lines to assume a more friendly disposition towards our interests, especially is this so in the damage suit cases."[34]

Organized education was used in several ways to increase
worker efficiency. Placing children in schools freed both parents
for work either in the factory or home. The Dean River Power
and Manufacturing Company of Danville, Virginia, reported
that it provided a day nursery after they realized the danger of
leaving the child unattended while the mother worked. It was
reported that the "need for a day nursery was evidenced by the
shocking discovery one day of the half-charred body of a little
child near one of the open fireplaces. . . . The nursery, now
thoroughly established, is a great success."[35]

Kindergartens were also regarded as a means of improving
the quality of the worker's home and consequently his physical and mental condition for work. The Plymouth Cordage
Company provided a trained kindergarten teacher and assistant
to take care of a class of forty kindergartners. The company
believed that by removing the children from the house for
part of the day the mother could give her undivided attention
to housework. The kindergartens also provided a way for the
teachers to get into the workers' houses. Tolman reported that
the kindergarten teachers at Plymouth Cordage "make visits
about the houses and interest the mothers in the children's
work."[36]

Education for workers' children was also supported in
terms of the long range objective of preparing a future labor
force. Tolman reminded employers, "The children are coming
into your shop in a very few years; how much better for you
that their bodies have been somewhat strengthened by exercise, and their minds disciplined by regulated play."[37] The
N. O. Nelson Company and Ludlow Manufacturing Associates
supported school systems specifically designed to produce workers for their companies. The idea behind the school system
supported by N. O. Nelson was the union of industrial training
with education from books. Between kindergarten and twelve
years of age the boys were taught, along with their regular
studies, the cultivation of vegetables and flowers and manual

arts. Boys at the age of twelve devoted one hour of work in either the factory or on the company's farm. As the boys grew older their hours of labor were increased and the time devoted to studies decreased. Upon reaching the age of eighteen they graduated from school and were employed full-time at the factory.[38] The Ludlow Manufacturing Associates arranged the school day so that half the time was spent in the factory. Classes were alternated between morning and afternoon so that the schoolhouse was always occupied.[39]

The National Cash Register Company exterted a large influence on the education of their employees' children. The N.C.R. house, or as it was called, the house of usefulness, provided three trained kindergarten teachers to influence the child in what was considered to be his most important stage of development. Tolman reported the philosophy of the N.C.R. kindergarten, "The Lessons of order and neatness, the discipline of regulated play . . . are acquisitions, making the child of greater value to himself, and, if he can follow up the good start which has been made for him, tending to make him of greater wage earning capacity. . . ." National Cash Register also tried to influence the local school system. The company used the influence of their factory-run Sunday school to convince the children to have their parents petition for a cooking and manual training school. The children were told that if they had training of that type when "they left school they would have an earning power of three or four dollars per day. . . . It was stated that two-thirds of the people who were out of work during the last panic were out on account of ill health, and that this might be overcome by teaching preventive hygiene; and that good cooking would make three dollars' worth of food go as far as six dollars' worth if badly cooked. . . ."[40] Patterson, the founder of N.C.R., believed that if the city in which the company is placed does not have an adequate system of education the factory must set an example. He was eventually responsible for the city of Dayton, Ohio, developing a complete system of kindergartens.[41]

Companies that employed large numbers of young workers often provided their own system of schooling. This was particularly true of large retailing houses. The Daniels & Fisher Stores Co. of Denver, Colorado, attempted to have all workers under the age of eighteen attend classes from 8:30 to 11:30 each day except Monday. In 1899 the enrollment was twenty girls and eighteen boys. They were divided into six divisions, and these six divisions united into four classes, each class reciting forty minutes. Textbooks were provided by the store. The course of study included history, reading, spelling, geography, and the discussion of current events. Each morning the teacher went through the newspaper explaining to the pupils the daily events and answering all questions. One reason retail companies could provide education during working hours was because of the small flow of business during the morning hours. It was believed that the time could be more profitably used during the morning to improve the quality of employees. Some stores devoted part of their time to teaching etiquette for more effective salesmanship. The Hochschild, Kohn & Company department store of Baltimore provided educational classes during store hours for boys between the ages of fourteen and eighteen. The instruction included mathematics, English, penmanship, reading, store etiquette, and commercial ethics. The value of these educational enterprises was attested to by a Mr. Letts of the Broadway department store school in Los Angeles. Letts wrote Tolman, "These boys and girls have demonstrated beyond question that owing to the training and discipline they have received through the school's instructions, they are equipped far in advance of the average department store employee." Letts went on to complain that his competitors used every known artifice to steal his better trained employees.[42]

One of the largest educational enterprises conducted by a retail store was that of the John Wanamaker's store in Philadelphia. The store employed a corps of twenty-two teachers who met with approximately three hundred older boys twice a week. The classes were conducted in the evening and all students were given a free meal by the store. The students were taught a commercial course which included English, arithmetic, stenography, bookkeeping, commercial geography, commercial law, and business methods. Formal instruction was not the only important feature of the evening school. The store also organized through its evening school a drum and bugle corps of 31 members, a military band of 50 members, an orches-tra of 17, and a uniformed cadet battalion of 210. All members of the school belonged to a literary club which gave training in recitation and public speaking. The whole evening school was also brought together in choral singing. A gymnasium session included calisthenics, United States Army setting-up drill, and military drill. The department store maintained a summer camp at Island Heights, New Jersey, where the boys were sent for two weeks during the summer. During the rest of the summer the camp was used by the older workers in the store. The total educational system was capped with an alumni asso-ciation of 420 members.[43]

Some companies organized classes and lectures for the general moral and social improvement of their employees. Em-ployers believed that there was a direct correlation between the moral and mental condition of their workers and job effi-ciency. E. A. Filene of Filene's department store reported that besides teaching their employees practical subjects, they had also brought in guest lecturers to teach color and line harmony and elementary psychology. John H. Patterson of National Cash Register had a collection of 7,000 lantern slides that he used to entertain and instruct his employees in geography, health, science, and mechanics. National Cash Register also offered a wide variety of courses including a dancing class with a re-ported attendance of 550 members in 1909. Bands and company choral societies became a popular way of occupying the em-ployee's time while uplifting his mental character and cement-ing his allegiance to the company. In 1907 Marshall Field and Company of Chicago gave a concert in the largest music hall in the city. The choral organization of the company was a select group. Prospective members had to pass examinations and at-tend special classes. It was quite common for company music groups to participate in public parades and concerts.[44]

With the development of highly complex industrial pro-cesses, corporations had to develop their own training programs for specific industrial skills. In 1902 the Westinghouse Corporation opened the Casino Technical Night School in East Pittsburgh. The school was within walking distance of the major plants of Westinghouse which employed 14,000 men. The school was open to the entire community but its courses were specifically directed toward production problems. The company did not claim to be giving a finished engineering course but just fundamental training in problems of electrical and steam engineering. Insurance companies, such as Metropolitan Life, offered instruction in higher mathematics without expense to their clerical force. Patterson at National Cash Register used some of his 7,000 slides to train factory mechanics. This type of corporate training was not directed to particular problems of social control or management but reflected a very practical need for people with specific skills.[45]

It can easily be assumed that corporations which developed their own cooking classes, kindergartens, physical training programs, literary activities, and trade classes would put pressure on their local communities to have the schools assume some of these functions. It was cheaper, of course, for corporations to have present and future workers trained at public expense. Corporations could also view these educational activities as being of benefit to the entire community. Certainly, if an employer was concerned about social strife and labor militancy, and if he believed that inability to handle the family budget and improper diet and cooking contributed to the worker's discontent, that employer would pressure the local school system into adopting homemaking and cooking courses. This type of corporate demand upon the schools was exemplified on a national scale by the activities of the National Association of Manufacturers. The National Association of Manufacturers passed resolution after resolution calling for high schools to teach modern languages and commercial courses and calling for the opening of trade schools. The N.A.M.'s interest in modern languages was the result of a general business interest in foreign trade. The president's opening report of the second annual meeting of the N.A.M. in 1897 stressed the importance of developing foreign markets particularly in South America. The N.A.M. president told the gathered businessmen that its South

American commission had investigated the trade conditions in Brazil and the River Platte countries and had found that "there is opportunity for a very large increase in the volume of our South American trade, and the means necessary to secure our share of this business which naturally belongs to us are clearly set forth." The president stressed to his audience that what had to be done to exploit these markets was to "send there competent salesmen who are able to speak Spanish or Portuguese and who are able to accommodate themselves to the conditions they find."[46]

It was the difficulty of finding Americans who were fluent in foreign languages that caused businessmen to demand that the schools teach modern languages and a commercial course that included a study of foreign customs. The N.A.M. passed a resolution in 1900 which argued that future prosperity of the country depended on "foreign trade and business of a complex character, and that to secure this end it is desirable to place within reach of the young facilities for securing comprehensive business education. . . ." The president's report in 1903 reaffirmed the position of the N.A.M. in support of commercial education and foreign languages because "the lack of men thoroughly conversant with the languages and customs of countries with which we seek to trade is a serious bar to commercial intercourse with them." The N.A.M. never felt that the schools were changing rapidly enough. The president reported in disgust in 1901 that he had written for a copy of a curriculum recently adopted in a high school and found that it provided for a general education but not for one that would meet the needs of business. He told the organization, "I have a strong conviction that there has been no step taken yet in this country in the commercial education of our young men that exactly fills the desires of the National Association of Manufacturers." The three languages that he wanted stressed in his ideal commercial curriculum were French, German, and Spanish.[47]

The N.A.M. supported trade schools primarily as a means of limiting the power of the developing labor movement. Unions wanted to control the apprenticeship systems as a means of assuring that future workers would be union members, consequently the unions resisted the early efforts made by the N.A.M. to establish trade schools. The N.A.M. wanted trade schools for the purpose of destroying union influence over trade training and because they felt that union control of the apprenticeship system was being used to maintain high wage levels by limiting the size of the skilled work force. The N.A.M. resolutions on trade schools developed a rather fanatical and tiresome tone between 1905 and 1914. The industrial education committee of the N.A.M. concluded its 1905 report recommending trade schools with the statement, "At no time since the dawn of economic history was there a greater or more far-reaching issue than that involved in this very question of giving the American boy the opportunity to win for himself and this nation economic liberty and personal freedom from domination by the labor combination. . . ."[48] The theme of saving the American boy from unionism echoed throughout the N.A.M.'s statements on education during this period. The Fifteenth Annual Convention of the N.A.M. in 1910 was opened with the prayer, "O Thou Great Manufacturer, greatest of all, Maker of trees and flowers, of soils and mountains and worlds, we take Thy material into our hands and try to make it more marketable among men." President Kirby then stressed that "trade schools . . . [are] more and more demanded as means of recruiting the ranks of skilled mechanics . . . as well as to checkmate militant organized labor on its policy of obstructing the free employment of apprentices."[49]

The American Federation of Labor was just as vehement in its denunciation of the type of trade school being promoted by the N.A.M. In 1908 the A.F. of L. formed its own committee of industrial education and warned that there were "non-union employers of the country who advance industrial education as a special privilege under conditions that educate the student or apprentice to non-union sympathies and prepare him as a skilled worker for scab labor and strike-breaking purposes. . . ."[50] There was basically little difference between the type of education advocated by both the N.A.M. and labor. The problem centered around control and the question of union indoctrination. Both groups agreed that education should be used to increase the productive capacity of the worker. As long as the N.A.M. rejected the idea of labor involvement in the trade school movement there was no hope of reconciliation. Statements by the president of the N.A.M. in 1911 that including labor in the trade school movement was like a "tarantula . . . on the bosom of an angel" did little to decrease the friction between the two groups.[51] The reconciliation did finally come in 1914 when the chairman of the N.A.M. committee on industrial education became H. E. Miles, president of the Board of Industrial Education of the State of Wisconsin. Miles accepted the idea of including labor on a Board of Industrial Education and this acceptance made it possible for labor and the N.A.M. to work together for the passage of the Smith-Hughes Bill in 1917.[52]

The general activites of N.A.M. reflected the value industrialists saw in the public school systems. Education could be used for job training and as a means of preparing the future worker for industrial management. The N.A.M.'s specific concern was with the influence of labor organizations over the general character of the worker. The more general concern of industrialists was that the schools produce an individual who was cooperative, knew how to work well with others, and was physically and mentally equipped to do his job efficiently. A cooperative and unselfish individual not only worked well with his fellows in the corporate organization but was also more easily managed.

This attitude was reflected by the National Association of Corporation Schools founded in 1913. Berenice Fisher has reported that these corporate educators wanted the public schools to provide a basic education which included not only languages and mathematics, but also a "curriculum broad enough to insure both 'vocational efficiency' and 'an insight into the social and moral needs of community life, cooperative action, and civic responsibility.' "[53]

CHAPTER THREE

THE CLASSROOM AS FACTORY AND COMMUNITY

The one great enemy of educational reformers at the end of the nineteenth century was the routine and mechanical atmosphere of the traditional classroom. In its place were offered teaching methods that stressed cooperative activity and personal interaction. There were three major reasons for these changes in classroom organization. One was the growing belief that the pupil learned more readily if the social value of the material were shown. Group activity in the classroom provided this opportunity. The second reason was that the traditional classroom reflected a factory system which alienated the student from his fellow pupils. This created a sense of selfish individualism that continued under the pressures of the modern urban and industrial society. The classroom had to be changed to counteract this negative aspect of modern life. Social activity in the schoolroom in this case was designed to give the pupil an understanding of the interdependence of society. When the student became a worker he would be able to give meaning to the fragmented experience of the industrialized world. The last and most dominant reason was preparation for an organized society. The child learned in cooperative activities how to get along with others. This was the most pervasive objective in socializing the work of the classroom. It often resulted in a rigid stress on social conformity.

The development of a factory-like system in the nineteenth century schoolroom was not accidental. The monitorial or Lancasterian system, the most popular and widespread educational method in the early part of the nineteenth century, was referred to by its chief promoter in the United States as "a system which is, in education, what the neat finished machines for abridging labor and expense are in the mechanic arts."[1] The system was introduced by the New York Free School Society during the opening decade of the century as an inexpensive and efficient method of educating large numbers of students. The method followed the lines of a factory model with knowledge being given to students on an assembly line basis. For instance, an engraving of an early Lancasterian classroom showed a large room holding 450 pupils that was divided into twelve sections with three of the sections in the front containing elliptical desks. The class was run by one master who sat on a raised platform in front of the class and by monitors assigned to each section. The monitors were selected from the best students who were trained to teach one particular part of the class work. The pupils during the course of the school day would march from one section to another receiving instruction from each monitor. The monitors were in essence just points on the educational assembly line.[2] One unidentified French writer aptly described it as a "masterpiece which must produce a revolution in popular education. . . . It may be styled a manufactory of knowledge. . . ."[3]

It was argued that the factory atmosphere of the Lancasterian system was ideal training for a developing industrial society. Movement from section to section and instruction in large numbers required orderliness and precise habits on the part of the students. Handbooks were written that gave detailed instruction in such things as passing out books. With large numbers of pupils, procedures of this nature required a high degree of organization. Training the child to be a cog in this type of machine was preparation for the routine of the industrial world. When the Boston School Committee investigated the New York Lancasterian Schools in 1828, it reported that "its effects on the habits, character, and intelligence of youth are highly beneficial; disposing their minds to industry, to readiness of attention, and to subordination, thereby creating in early life a love of order, preparation for business. . . ."[4]

Utilization of the classroom for training industrial habits continued into the twentieth century. The mechanical class routine was perpetuated by certain educational leaders such as William Bagley. Bagley's book, *Classroom Management*, became a standard teacher training text during the first quarter of the century and was reprinted thirty times between 1907 and 1927. Bagley was fully aware that criticisms were being made of mechanical routine. In his book he defined the two positions on classroom management as being machine-like organization and self-government. Bagley dismissed the self-government approach as being inefficient. He supported machine-like organization because, "One who studies educational theory aright can see in the mechanical routine of the classroom the educative forces that are slowly transforming the child from a little savage into a creature of law and order, fit for the life of civilized society."[5]

Bagley's theory of classroom management was directly related to what he called the major objective of education, social efficiency. The socially efficient man was for Bagley one who could earn his own livelihood and who "sacrifices his own pleasure when this interferes with the productive efforts of his fellows. . . ."[6] The training in Bagley's classroom was preparation for becoming an efficient and productive worker on an industrial assembly line. The important job of the school was to build good industrial habits. Bagley's ideal teacher was one who would "rigidly 'hew to the line' in all of these initial stages of habit-building. Even scholarship could be sacrificed, if necessary, in attaining this end." Everything within the school had to be reduced to rigid routine. Bagley wrote that the expert observer could immediately gauge the efficiency of the teacher by "the manner in which lines pass to and from the room." Since Bagley could find no arguments against pupils keeping step while walking, he advocated the Lancasterian method of lock-step marches. He also insisted that students be given drills in packing their desks in a certain order, in going to assigned places at the blackboard, in leaving the room, and in marching through the cloakroom to collect wraps. To reduce the problem of children interrupting class activities he wrote that "regular habits should be speedily established with regard to the bodily functions." One method he suggested was that "the lines [be] passed to the latrines and closets at each recess before being allowed to go upon the playground . . . this will gradually control the difficulty." Bagley also argued that psychology had shown that an attentive attitude of mind was closely related to an attentive attitude of the body. Therefore, he reasoned, the teacher should train his students to give physical attention upon command. "In general, the command, Attention! should be the stimulus for the habitual adjustment of the body in a certain definite posture. . . ." Bagley suggested "head erect, eyes turned toward the teacher, hands or arms folded (preferably the former), feet flat on the floor, instant cessation of all their school work or activity."[7]

The objections raised to this type of classroom were very similar to those leveled at the effect of the factory on the worker. The work of the mechanical classroom isolated the individual from the rest of the members of the class. Working at a desk on one independent project never gave the student an opportunity to interact with his fellow pupils. William Heard Kilpatrick's statement in 1918 was typical of this feeling that the traditional classroom separated the individual from the group. Kilpatrick wrote that "the tendency toward selfish individualism [was] one of the strongest counts against our customary set-task sit-alone-at-your-own-desk."[8] Similar criticisms were even leveled at common practices, such as silent reading. "Studying alone out of a book," for instance, was considered by the Francis Parker School as "an isolated and unsocial performance; the pupils may be learning the words before him, but he is not learning to act with other people. . . ."[9]

There was also concern over whether the traditional classroom did in fact create independent thinking. About the only argument given by defenders to support independent activity in the classroom was that it developed self-initiative and individual abilities. This was strongly denied by those who offered a new form of classroom organization. Colin Scott, who became the great propagandist for socialized group activity in the classroom, felt that uniformity, and not independent thinking, was the result of traditional methods. "Owing," he wrote, "to the pressure of outside social sentiment, independent thinking is usually held up as a great virtue in education. . . ." The teacher to accomplish this insists that the work be done independently at separate desks or if at home, uses honor codes and threats to keep the students from communicating. In Scott's opinion the end result of this preparation for independent thought was completed exercises that were "strangely uniform." According to Scott this had, after all, been the original aim of the teacher.[10]

Criticisms raised about the traditional reliance upon grades and rewards followed the similar pattern of concern about breeding selfish individualism. A reward system had been an important part of the mechanical system. Rewards had functioned as a sort of wage system based on quantity and quality of work. The Lancasterian system had an elaborate system of rewards ranging from badges, the highest being the Order of Merit, to appointment to the important post of monitor. Using rewards in the classroom was objected to on the grounds that they fostered competitiveness and conditioned the individual to work for his own interests and not for the good of society. One writer in the *Educational Review* in 1902 argued that if the social ideal of mutual cooperation and dedication to the common good were to be accomplished, all prizes, awards, and competition would have to be removed from the classroom. These stimulants to competition were just concessions to modern commercialism. The competitive spirit in the classroom, he wrote, should be replaced by a "functional pleasure in acquiring and using knowledge, and the gratification which always comes from successful co-operation towards a worthy end."[11] The effort was being made to change classroom motivation from self-interest to social goals. The Francis Parker School, for instance, attempted to develop teaching methods that would train the student to be motivated by group and not individual interests. Their first yearbook in 1912 was called *The Social Motive in School Work* and stated "that the motive of the individual's activities is a dominating factor of importance to his activities . . . and that the motive of work must not be the advancement of self as against another. . . ." The Parker School's alternative to competition and personal aggrandizement was the substitution of "the social motive as an ever present, powerful, active force, inspiring and producing in all the pupils the best that in them lies."[12]

Grades were considered socially divisive because they created an artificial sense of superiority and inferiority. William McAndrew, superintendent of the New York schools, wrote in 1912 that one "unsocial custom persisting from feudal times is the award of prizes for superiority in scholarship. There is no social service secured by the selection of the best scholar for special honor. It is rank individualism."[13] Grades in this case created a system of social classes in the schoolroom which led to the domination of class activities by the superior students. This was one concern voiced by Samuel T. Dutton in a collection of lectures he published in 1899. The lectures had been given at the universities of Chicago, Harvard, and Boston while Dutton was superintendent of schools in Brookline, Massachusetts. Dutton asked his audiences, "It the acquisition of knowledge of such tremendous importance that the social code is to be constantly violated in the schoolroom? Is it not often that, in a given recitation, a few brilliant pupils are permitted to do all the work, and that, too, with an air of superiority which in the highest degree is unsocial? Dutton's answer was to reorganize the classroom so that mutual assistance and cooperation would occur.[14]

The most widespread attempt to correct for the individualistic tendencies of the classroom was through the introduction of group activities. The industrial and urban society was functioning to break down relationships between people causing a loss of a sense of community and an ability to cooperate. Education was useless as a corrector of social problems if it were also guilty of alienation. The function of group activities was to shift the work of the classroom from individual effort and competition to group work and group achievement. The objective was to educate people who would know how to cooperate and work with others.

The two men who provided the theoretical framework and popularized the idea of group work in the classroom were John Dewey and Colin Scott. Both reacted to the social and economic conditions of the period and both felt that a sense of community had to be restored. The major disagreement between the two was over the implementation of educational theory. Scott agreed with Dewey's diagnosis of society and with his educational theories. Where Scott felt Dewey failed was in developing his theory into a practical and useful method.

John Dewey's two major educational objectives when he founded the laboratory school at the University of Chicago in 1896 were to make the student aware of the social value and relationships of the subject matter and to help the pupil become aware of his place and function in society. One way Dewey hoped to achieve these two objectives was through the development of social imagination in cooperative group activity. What Dewey meant by social imagination was "the habit of mentally constructing some actual scene of human interaction, and of consulting that for instruction as to what to do." One of Dewey's early experiments was in a high school ethics class in the early part of the 1890's. In this particular case Dewey wanted the students to become aware that the study of ethics was not an abstract subject but involved real problems in social relationships. What Dewey suggested was that students be presented with an actual case of human misery to work out the problem of charity. Social imagination involved the ability to relate isolated ideas to the actual conditions which had given them their original meaning. Dewey argued that this method aided in forming within the student "the habit of realizing for himself and in himself the nature of the practical situations in which he will find himself placed."[15]

Dewey did not feel that it was enough to just make the student aware of these relationships. Opportunity had to be provided for students to act upon their ideas. It was Dewey's conviction that the product of social imagination remained as mere information until acted upon. When acted upon, it became judgment. "The child," Dewey stated, "cannot get power of judgment excepting as he is continually exercised in forming and testing judgment."[16] Therefore the school, as Dewey saw it, must provide the child not with abstract ideas but with actual conditions out of which ideas grow. The child must be given an opportunity within the school to test his moral and social judgments. This meant that the school had to become a community of real social relations.

One of the most often quoted statements made by Dewey was that the school was a community with a real social life. What Dewey wanted was to utilize this community and make it a part of the learning process. From Dewey's point of view knowledge was a product of social conditions. The learning process, Dewey felt, should be a part of an active solution to a social problem. This, he believed, provided the best basis for learning and helped the student to see the social value of the subject. Counting, for instance, was introduced to children at the Dewey School in the context of a real social problem. Nursery children in the school had the responsibility of setting the table for the mid-morning snack. The children quickly learned that there was a problem in matching the number of utensils with the number of pupils.[17]

Dewey hoped that children working in the context of a school community would learn habits of order, industry, and cooperation. These were habits that were not being taught to the child by the modern urbanized and industrialized society. In 1899 when John Dewey delivered his School and Society lectures in response to criticisms of his educational work, he stressed the point that the march of industrialism had destroyed a household and community life that had given the child "training in habits of order and of industry, and in the idea of responsibility of obligation to produce something in the world." These habits had been learned in the past when most occupations centered around the household. Dewey reminded his audience in industrial Chicago that "those of us who are here today need go back only one, two, or at most three generations, to find a time when the household was practically the center . . . [of] all the typical forms of industrial occupation." It was Dewey's contention that the child at one time had helped the family make clothes, candles, soap, and other household necessities. Articles not manufactured in the home were usually produced in the immediate neighborhood. Dewey interpreted this situation to mean that the child experienced and participated in the total industrial process of the community. From these community experiences the child learned moral habits, industry, and social cooperation. "But," Dewey said, "it is useless to bemoan the departure of the good old days of children's modesty, reverence, and implicit obedience. . . ." The problem, Dewey stated, was to retain the advantages of the present and at the same time introduce "into the school something representing the other side of life—occupations which exact personal responsibilities and which train the child in relation to the physical realities of life. . . ."[18]

The work that went on in the Dewey School in Chicago was designed to create social interaction between the pupils that would foster efficient learning and good social habits. The activity of the younger members of the school centered around household occupations. Work directed toward a common productive end, Dewey believed, created an atmosphere of community. Children between the ages of four and five were given the responsibility of preparing their own mid-morning luncheons. The children discussed their own home life and were led to explore marketing, mail service, and other related occupations. The children played at making a dry goods store which provided them with the opportunity to develop habits of industry, responsibility, and social cooperation. They were also learning as a basic part of these activities reading, writing, and arithmetic. These were skills that were needed to complete the projects.

As the children progressed, they were led to ever widening circles of activity. At age six the children were introduced to the activities of the farm. They built a farm house and barn out of blocks and explored the problems of climate and prod-

ucts. At age seven they began to study the historical development of mankind. This was a theme that persisted throughout
the rest of their stay at the Dewey School. At all times activity
was associated with their work. The children began their study
of history by investigating historical occupations. The children
engaged in activities such as weaving and building smelters.
The study of history was spiraled so that as the child progressed he came into broader contact with the social history of
mankind.[19]

The study of history was directly related to Dewey's ideas
on social imagination and community. The child developed his
social imagination by learning to relate ideas, inventions, and
institutions to the conditions which gave birth to them. This
process also made the pupil aware of the interdependence of
society. This habit of social imagination was the key to Dewey's
idea of community. "A society," Dewey said, "is a number of
people held together because they are working along common
lines, in a common spirit, and with references to common
ends."[20] Dewey felt that the community of America's past was
a genuine community because the individual was aware of the
total industrial process.

Dewey's stress upon group activities was directly related to
a belief that the existing industrial and urban society isolated
the individual. For Dewey America was becoming a society
where people were not held together by an awareness of
common ends. The function of social imagination learned in
cooperative activity was to help the individual relate his work
to the total industrial process and be made aware of the
common ends of social action. Facing his audience of critics in
Chicago in 1899 Dewey stated, "How many of the employed
are today mere appendages to the machines which they operate! This . . . is certainly due in large part to the fact that the
worker has had no opportunity to develop his imagination and
his sympathetic insight as to the social and scientific values
found in his work."[21] In 1902, before the National Education
Association, Dewey argued that the school should be the center
around which a genuine community life was maintained in
urban America. Supporting the idea of the school as a social

center he argued that "it must interpret to [the worker] the intellectual and social meaning of the work in which he is engaged: that is, must reveal its relations to the life and work of the world."[22]

Developing social imagination and using historical occupations were not the ideas that other educators got from Dewey's work. What they concentrated on was Dewey's stress on the importance of social activity as a basic method of education. Statements made by Dewey, such as, "the true center of correlation on the school subjects is . . . the child's own social activities,"[23] were used to support a variety of educational methods that stressed group and social activity in the schools. Often these methods placed an emphasis on group conformity that went beyond anything Dewey intended. For instance, Dewey believed that motives and choices did grow out of social situations, but he did not believe, as many other educators were to argue, that individual motives and goals should conform to the wishes of the group. Dewey wanted to free individual action, not submerge it to the mediocre standard of group consensus.

Essentially what Dewey wanted to do was give meaning to the fragmented experiences of the world of modern man. Colin Scott, on the other hand, wanted to organize the classroom around cooperative group activities because he felt that this was the way society was organized. Ideally the state functioned at maximum efficiency when organized into groups "in which each individual in various groups to which he may belong, finds himself in contact with others whose weaknesses he supplements or whose greater powers he depends upon."[24] Training to work in groups was for the promotion of the maximum efficiency of society. The traditional classroom atmosphere ran counter to this form of social organization. Scott believed that training in the classroom to initiate group projects would prepare the child to enter society and form similar cooperative groups.

Scott's failure to understand the role of social imagination led him to accuse Dewey of an "irreconcilable gap" between theory and practice. According to Scott they both agreed that the defects of the typical school were "its emphasis on the mere absorption of facts by uncooperative individuals, its competitive standards of success, the negative character of its discipline. . . ." Both also agreed that the school must be organized as a community and the spirit of community activity must be inculcated into the child. What Scott could not understand was why Dewey emphasized historical occupations. Scott did not evaluate these activities in terms of social imagination but in terms of how much they trained the child for group life. Evaluation on this basis led Scott to accuse Dewey of the gap between theory and practice. Since the historical occupations were planned by the teachers, they did not give the student any real sense of initiating a group project and being responsible for its completion. Scott wrote that "children who are weaving mats under the direction of a teacher cannot fail. They may not succeed with the mats, and they may be disappointed as a result; but the responsibility is that of the teacher, and the success of the undertaking depends on his inspiration, on his judgment and sense."[25]

What Scott offered as a means of training the student for group life was what he called self-organized group activity in the classroom. Scott developed this idea while working in schools in the West at the beginning of the century. He later used his position as head of the department of psychology of the Boston Normal School to conduct group experiments in the schools around Boston. In 1906 he organized the Social Education Association as a vehicle for his ideas on social training. The organization attracted a large number of people interested in social education including department store owners and librarians. While the association reflected a broad spectrum of ideas on social education, its objective was in agreement with Scott's general goals. The charter of the association stated "that the fundamental purpose of education should be to prepare the child for a useful life of social service as an active and creative member of the social organism."[26]

Self-organized group activity allowed children in the classroom to choose their own goals, organize their own groups, and delegate the work amongst themselves. In one example cited by Scott, a class at the Chicago and Cook County Normal School was asked, "If you had time given to you for something that you enjoy doing, and that you think worthwhile, what should you choose to do?" Three boys immediately hit upon the idea of printing. They formed a printing group and began publishing material for the class. In another class in the same school the formation of a printing group was promptly bogged down by an overabundance of members. The teacher told them that if they were unable to accomplish their purpose they would have to give up their project. Scott reported, "They had a little consultation among themselves, and decided that there were too many in the group for the work to be done . . . the group was thinned by its own action, and the work was finished successfully." During the year 1901-1902 Scott performed similar experiments at the Colorado Normal School. At Colorado he showed how self-organized groups could be utilized in an ordinary class such as American history. In this particular case the class was turned over to the students to organize in any manner. What happened was that the class divided itself into the Senate and House of Representatives, selected a student to be government printer, and studied history as a series of legislative bills and debates. The value that Scott saw in this work was that it taught the students how to organize an efficient group that utilized the individual talents of the members of the class.[27]

Scott's emphasis on group activities as preparation for a more efficient social organization became characteristic of the arguments for social education in the classroom. It represented an important shift from Dewey's thinking. Social education within this context became more coercive and demanded that the child learn to cooperate and get along with others. With Dewey cooperation was a means to an end. For Scott and other social educators, group cooperation was the end. This meant that the school assumed the function and obligation of making people get along with each other. The role of the school was to impose a sense of social obligation and dependency on group activity. Scott fully accepted this idea of the coercive nature of the school when he wrote, "It is not primarily for his own individual good that the child is taken from his free and wandering life of play. It is for what society can get out of him, whether of a material or a spiritual kind, that he is sent to school."[28] What Scott felt society should get out of a child's education was a cooperating member of society.

The result of this coercive approach was to make self-organized group activity into a method of conditioning the individual to conform to group standards. Scott argued that all school work should be evaluated by a social standard. Even reading was to be viewed in the context of its total social value and use. He warned, "The procession of gaunt bookworms that crawls forth from the British Museum every evening when the doors close have acquired the reading habit, but very few of them have acquired anything else."[29] In the same manner evaluation of school work had to be in terms of social standards. Scott proposed a system of cooperative grading by which students every six weeks would determine how much each pupil contributed to the class. According to Scott's plan the pupils would sit in a circle and each student would be called before the group. The pupils would try to determine how much each student contributed to his own individual advancement in knowledge. The student would then be credited with every distinct contribution he had made to the group. The student's grades would be based on total contributions.[30]

After Dewey's and Scott's work, the idea of socialized classroom instruction became widespread. Articles in educational journals and books on group classroom activities appeared in large numbers. The topics ranged from socializing arithmetic drills to teaching cooking with self-organized groups. At Teachers College, William Heard Kilpatrick used his classes in educational theory to teach a form of group learning called the project method. His article on the method first printed in 1918 became so popular and widely used that it went through seven impressions by 1922. Following the lead of education professors like Michael V. O'Shea at the University of Wisconsin and Irving King at the University of Iowa, courses in social education began to be offered in teacher training programs. King had been one of Dewey's students at Chicago.

Both King and O'Shea published textbooks that emphasized the importance of social training. King's first textbook on the subject, *Social Aspects of Education*, was published in 1912 and was an anthology of writings ranging from Dewey and Scott on cooperative school work to articles on social anthropology. This book was followed in 1913 by *Education for Social Efficiency* which devoted a section on classroom method to Colin Scott. Other very practical books on socialized recitation appeared on the book market. Many of these worked out in elaborate detail classroom procedures for encouraging group work.

The continuing themes of socialized classroom work tended to be more like Scott's than Dewey's. The concern over giving added meaning to modern life was lost in the efforts to create more efficient learning conditions and to prepare for efficient group activity outside of the school. These motives almost inevitably led to concentration on classroom techniques that emphasized conformity to group standards.

Irving King was one example of those who continued the argument that society functioned most efficiently when organized into corporate groups. According to King's view of social organization, group work represented something different than the sum of each individual's work. The organization of the group could either add to or detract from the work. The important thing for educators was to remember that the different members of a group "may interfere with each other through lack of proper coordination of the individual efforts. They may also actually help one another to do more." The function of the school was to create classroom conditions that taught the students how to effectively utilize the strengths of group organization. One example he gave of a rather typical socialized classroom technique was of a history class that elected a president and secretary and conducted their lessons in the form of a town meeting. The class would begin with the reading of minutes and then the lesson for the day would be called for. Students would rise and in parliamentary fashion give the lesson. King wrote about the experiment conducted by Lotta A. Clark of the Charlestown (Massachusetts) High School that it was "the spirit of such undertakings that be imitated. . . ." The spirit in this case was "the material of personal intercourse."[31]

Group instruction as an efficient method of teaching was premised on the idea that learning would take place more readily if the student saw the social value of his work. This, of course, had been one of the basic concepts of Dewey's work. Clark, for instance, had defended her work with the history classes by asking, "Do our lessons in grammar make our boys and girls speak good English at home, in the street, or even in the classroom? How many of our boys in school learn to add and subtract as our newsboys do on the street?"[32] Classroom activities were to be organized to make the learning of skill subjects, such as reading, writing, and arithmetic, a part of a natural group activity. One writer summed up this method in a 1907 article titled, "Socializing the Materials and Methods of Education," as cultivating "through construction (all forms of actual as opposed to symbolic doing) the social values of, the social estimate of, and the social attitude toward, the [school] materials dealt with."[33]

The socially purposeful act was the heart of William Heard Kilpatrick's project method. What the purposeful act simply meant was an activity directed toward a socially useful end. As an example Kilpatrick cited the situation of a girl making a dress. The act of making a dress was a project if the girl was motivated by a social purpose and if she planned and made the dress. According to Kilpatrick the purposeful act was the basic unit of the worthy life and democracy. He wrote, "A man who habitually so regulates his life with reference to worthy social aims meets at once the demands for practical efficiency and of moral responsibility. Such a one presents the ideal of democratic citizenship."[34] Within the classroom children were prepared for a purposeful life by pursuing projects that grew out of social situations.

Kilpatrick's project method also reflected the social conformity inherent in most of the social education proposals. He considered moral character to be one of the important results of the project method. Moral character was defined as "the disposition to determine one's conduct and attitudes with reference to the welfare of the group." Development of this disposition within the classroom was through reliance on group acceptance and rejection. Kilpatrick based his argument on Thorndike's stimulus-response theory of learning. The learning experience was described in terms of establishing bonds between stimulus and response through reward. The reward in Kilpatrick's classroom was group approval. He stressed the idea that "there are few satisfactions so gratifying and few annoyances so distressing as the approval and disapproval of our comrade. . . . When the teacher merely coerces and the other pupils side with their comrade . . . conformity may be but outward. But when all concerned take part in deciding what is just . . . conformity is not merely outward."[35] According to Kilpatrick moral character was developed when the individual was conditioned to respond at all times to the desires of the group.

Conditioning to respond to group judgments was often considered realistic training for the corporate world. One book, *The Socialized Recitation,* published in 1915, stated with regard to a socialized arithmetic period, "In a small but growing way [the student] learns to hold his own in a junior business world, to be self-reliant, to listen even pleasantly to just interruptions and objections." As preparation for this junior business world, the author suggested that the pupil learn to "prove his conclusions to a group rather than to a single individual!" The writer offered as suggestions arithmetic games which included addition drills where the rest of the class judged individual performances.[36]

Socialized education as it spread through the American schools continued to be viewed as a method by which unity and a sense of community could be instilled in future American citizens. But there was one important qualitative difference between Dewey's original work and later statements on social unity. Dewey had wanted to replace the mechanical atmosphere of the classroom with social activity so that social unity would be the result of social understanding. Later methods of organizing group projects and creating a spirit of cooperative endeavor in the schoolroom tried to achieve unity through reliance on the social pressure of the group. Essentially what was to happen was that the individual was to lose his own personal identity to the group. One author wrote that the first objective of socialized recitation was the "development of a feeling which binds the members of a group in such a way as to make them a unit." By "feeling" the author meant that which "makes the individual regard himself a real part of the group and which causes him to identify his interest with group interests while he looks upon the common motives, purposes, and activities as ours rather than as mine."[37] A phrase that really captured the spirit of what was happening was used by a high school teacher in Lincoln, Nebraska, in 1921. The teacher wrote in praise of socialized recitation because it prepared the student for a society that demanded "a sort of social like-mindedness."[38]

The development of "social like-mindedness" did reflect the needs of a highly organized society. Like factory welfare programs, it was designed to counteract the alienation caused by the growing corporate organization of industrialism and urbanism. This was particularly reflected in the movement's attack on the organization of the traditional classroom as separating the individual from the group. The ultimate failure of the goal of social education in the classroom was that it wanted to impose a sense of unity rather than have the feeling of community grow out of the work. The result of this form of group education was an "organization man" who functioned well in the new corporate state because of "social like-mindedness" and not because of social imagination. Group learning experiences in the form of cooperative projects and socialized recitation prepared the individual to be what David Riesman called in later years "other-directed." Motivation and rewards were to become contingent on the approval of others.

CHAPTER FOUR

EXTENDING THE SOCIAL ROLE OF THE SCHOOL

I

Public education was able to fulfill the needs of the corporate state for specialized training and an education that inculcated the values of cooperation and identity with the corporate structure because more and more of the social training of the American child had come under the control of the school. Paralleling the development of the philosophy of the corporate state was an increasing expansion of the institutional activities of American public education. Education during the nineteenth century had been increasingly viewed as an instrument of social control to be used to solve the social problems of crime, poverty, and Americanization of the immigrant. The activities of the public school tended to replace the social training role of other institutions, such as the family and church. One reason for the extension of school activities was the concern for the education of the great numbers of immigrants arriving from eastern and southern Europe. It was feared that without some form of Americanization immigrants would cause a rapid decay of American institutions. An example of this attitude was a statement by the president-general of one educational group, the Sons of the American Revolution. In 1891 he stated, "With unrestricted immigration and hurried naturalization, it behooves all good Americans to awaken to the fact that we must take a more active part in the administration of our affairs. . . . Let us all work together with one object, one aim in view, and that is to Americanize our immigrants, and if they do not wish it, then we do not want them. . . ."[1]

The impact of immigrant education was particularly felt in the development of evening centers. Immigrant groups, crowded into the tenements of the large cities, could be brought together in school buildings after working hours for education in Americanization. A 1906 article in the *American Journal of Sociology* claimed that in 1903 there were ten thousand people enrolled in Chicago evening schools. Seventy percent of them were foreign born. In New York in 1902 the author estimated that evening and vacation schools had an attendance equivalent to one quarter of the regular daytime enrollment.

The author of the article gave three immediate reasons for this increased use of school property. One reason was the education of adult foreigners. Another, the writer stated, "arose from the side of need. To the children in the crowded parts of great cities, vacation does not mean grass and trees and hills and streams . . . but long hours on hot busy, bare streets or alleys. . . ." Vacation schools would save the child from summer harm and evening centers would provide a place for useful after-school activities. The author wrote that, "to the child so situated [in the city] the close of school is a time of peril." Lastly, there was a need for a place where young adults could engage in wholesome recreation and be saved from the saloons and commercial dance halls.[2]

Another reason for the extension of school activities was a strong anti-urban feeling. Urban education was often defined as the saving of the child from contact with the urban environment. This attitude was reflected early in the nineteenth century when in 1805 the New York Free School Society began its campaign to extend educational opportunities to the urban poor by literally going out into the streets and rounding up children for its schools. New York at that time had a population of 60,000 which by later standards would not be considered a teeming metropolis. But in the eyes of the president of the

Free School Society, De Witt Clinton, it was large enough to easily lead a child down the path of temptation. He warned in 1809, "Great cities are, at all times, the nurseries and hot-beds of crimes. . . . And the dreadful examples of vice which are presented to youth, and the alluring forms in which it is arrayed . . . cannot fail of augmenting the mass of moral depravity."[3] The goal of the Free School Society was to remove the child from the bad environment of the city streets, and place him in the moral atmosphere of a monitorial school.

By the 1890's the urban problem was considered to be not only the evil influence of the streets but also that of tenement living. The tenement building that came to dominate the urban landscape in the latter part of the nineteenth century was considered one of the major sources of moral decay. The most common form of building during this period was the "dumb-bell" tenement. The plan for this building was the result of a contest held in 1878 for the best design of a tenement on a 25 × 100 foot lot. The building was shaped like a dumb-bell having five to six stories with each floor containing fourteen rooms. When the arms of the dumb-bell were connected to the arms of the next building, the result was a narrow shaft. The shaft was originally presumed to be humane because it provided air and open space for all rooms. Actually, the shaft, which was only fifty-six inches wide, destroyed all privacy by conducting the noise of twenty or more families, proved a fire hazard, and collected garbage thrown from the tenement windows. It also doomed a great number of tenement dwellers to dingy apartments that never received adequate natural lighting and whose ventilation consisted of the stale odors of the shaft.[4] One little girl was asked in the 1890's if the sun's rays ever entered her apartment. "Yes it did," she said. "Once every summer, for a little while, it came over the houses." She knew the exact hour and day that the rays shone into her apartment.[5]

The concern with tenement living tended to emphasize the romantic pastoralism of American anti-urban feeling. The problem was not only the crowded conditions of city living but also its remoteness from the beneficial qualities of nature. The dinginess of tenement life magnified this remoteness. In terms of education this meant not only removing the child from the street but also assuring that he came into contact with nature.

The man who turned America's attention to the problems of tenement living was a New York newspaper reporter, Jacob Riis. Riis published in 1890 a best-selling book that conveyed the tragedy and horror of the slums of New York. The book was written in a journalistic style in which the bare facts of the case were to wring from the reader's heart a cry of sympathy. Riis took his reader from the Blind Man's alley where the "dirt was so thick on the walls, it smothered the fire" to dark attics where women starved to death while sewing from 4 A.M. to 11 P.M. The only sentimentality that showed through was for the tenement children. Riis wrote of the "little coffins . . . stacked mountain-high on the deck of the Charity Commissioners' boat when it makes its semi-weekly trips to the city cemetery" and told his reader "that the rescue of the children is the key to the problem of city poverty. . . ." For Riis the rescue of the child depended upon removing the child from the streets and providing him with a healthy antidote to the dark tenement.[6] In a book written ten years later, after conducting his own war with urban poverty, he wrote, "The way to fight the slum in the children's lives is with sunlight and flowers and play, which their child hearts crave, if their eyes have never seen them."[7]

One educational movement that attempted to solve some of these urban problems was the vacation or summer school. One of the first reported places to propose a vacation school was Cambridge, Massachusetts. In 1872 its school committee reported the need for a vacation school because summer was "a time of idleness, often of crime, with many who are left to roam the streets, with no friendly hand to guide them, save that of the police." Fifteen years later the superintendent of the same school district was still asking for a summer school as an inexpensive form of police. He wrote in his school report in 1897, "The value of these schools consists not so much in what shall be learned during the few weeks they are in session, as in the fact that no boy or girl shall be left with unoccupied time. Idleness is an opportunity for evil-doing. . . . These schools will cost money. Reform schools also cost money. . . ."[8] The first vacation school to be established was in Boston in 1885. This was followed by New York in 1894 and Cleveland and Brooklyn in 1897. In 1898 Chicago established what became a model vacation school system.

The Chicago vacation schools were opened in the most densely populated areas of the city. They limited enrollment by putting it on a first come, first served basis. The principal of the system reported that they were received with such enthusiasm that at "one of the schools it was found necessary to call in the police to remove the parents who crowded the halls of the building, insisting that their children must be accepted." At another school fifty of the children were held up on their way to school and their cards of admission taken from them. Some of the parents felt frustrated by the non-academic purpose of the school and withdrew their children after several weeks. The principal wrote about these parents that "their children had failed to make the grade [during the regular school year], and they thought they might make up the work in the summer." The thing that made Chicago a model system was its curriculum. It was designed by John Dewey and included both excursions to the country and work in "nature study, drawing and painting from nature, music, gymnastics and games, sewing and manual training."[9] The item in the curriculum that struck the imagination of reformers was the country excursions. Riis, writing in New York, stated that their vacation schools "took a hint from Chicago" and took the children into the country.[10] In Chicago when the first group of slum children got off the railroad at the end of the line, they crawled on their hands and knees to feel the country soil for the first time. The principal described how it was pathetic "to see the children rush for the ill-smelling and dusty chickweed of the roadside."[11]

One alternative to taking the children to the country was to bring a little bit of the country into the city. The development of parks and playgrounds to cure urban social problems in the United States began with small sandlots for children in the 1880's and reached a high point in the establishment of the Chicago park system in 1904. The prime motive for establishing parks and playgrounds was to reduce crime by keeping the children off the streets and by providing them with a healthy place to play. Sandlots were constructed in congested areas of Boston, Chicago, Philadelphia, and New York City between 1885 and 1895. These plays areas were designed for small children under twelve years of age and usually included a kindergarten program. One student of the movement reported the dominant motive for establishing sand parks was "to keep children off the street and out of mischief and vice."[12]

During the 1890's the playground movement expanded to include the ideas of providing play areas for older children and parks for adults so they could escape the closeness of tenement living. In New York Jacob Riis fought to have some of the worst tenements destroyed and replaced by large open areas. In 1890 Riis reported Mulberry Bend as the "foul core of New York's slums" and "a vast human pig-sty."[13] Through Riis's efforts the city bought the slums in the area in 1894 and in 1895 destroyed them and built a park. Riis in 1900 wrote with amazement that not fifteen years ago a murder would take place every Sunday in Mulberry Bend and now with the park the area was relatively free of crime. Riis reflected that it "is not that the murder has moved to another neighborhood. . . . It is that the light has come in and made crime hideous. It is being let in wherever the slum has bred murder and robbery, bred the gang, in the past."[14]

Included in the development of small parks was the construction of elaborate recreational and bathing facilities. These facilities were to provide both adults and children with healthy and morally sound physical activities. The motivation for providing these facilities was neatly summarized in a report of the Committee on Small Parks in New York City. This 1897 report claimed, "Crime in our large cities is to a great extent simply a question of athletics."[15] The bath movement was directed toward providing both recreation and an opportunity for the slum dweller to shed the dirt of the tenement. In 1898 the City of Boston created a bath department as a part of its city administration. The bath department had control of the city beaches, the floating baths, and municipal bath-houses.

The floating baths were floating platforms which supported a row of dressing rooms around an open space of water. In 1899 Boston had fourteen floating baths along with two swimming pools and seven shower baths in their municipal gymnasiums. In New York floating baths were started in 1876 and by 1889 there were fifteen. A campaign was waged in New York in the 1890's to increase the number of shower baths available. These were considered more suitable because they could be used during the winter. In 1900 New York had plans for the construction of a municipal building which would offer a tub or shower bath to 2,000 men and 900 women a day. Along with the movement for public baths was one for school baths. The first reported school bath was a shower opened in a Boston school in 1889. By 1900 all major cities in the country reported the development of both municipal and school bathing facilities.[16] The model playground of the period was the Charles Bank outdoor gymnasium in Boston. It had an average daily attendance of 1,500 and provided "196 lockers, a general shower-bath room with five rain showers and nine sprays, hot and cold water."[17]

In 1906 the Playground and Recreation Association of America was organized in Washington, D.C. Its honorary president and vice-president were Theodore Roosevelt and Jacob Riis. The founding of this organization symbolized the extreme progress that was being made in the construction of park and recreation facilities. In 1907 the association held it first Play Congress in Chicago in honor of the tremendous park system that Chicago had initiated in 1905. The Chicago park system involved the construction of ten parks centered around large field houses. The field houses contained separate gyms for both males and females, clubrooms, showers, locker rooms, and a branch of the public library. The outdoor facilities included a children's playground, a wading and a swimming pool, separate outdoor gyms for men and women, a music court, a theatrical stage, and a public restaurant.[18]

In 1917 Henry S. Curtis, one of the key organizers of the Playground and Recreation Association and former supervisor of the playgrounds of the District of Columbia, summarized the reasons for the widespread movement for establishing playgrounds and parks in the United States. One reason that Curtis gave was the need for physical exercise. Curtis argued that children confined to schools and adults trapped in factories and businesses needed the opportunity to exercise their bodies. Also, the increase in urban living had subjected people to nervous strain. People in urban areas needed fresh air and exercise to avoid "the rapid increase of insanity and the growing instability of the nervous system. . . ." But, Curtis wrote, "it has not been these reasons that have weighed most strongly with the people that have promoted the movement...." Curtis stated that the dominant motive and major concern of the leaders of the play movement was that there was "little for the children to do in the cities, and that in this time of idleness the devil has found much for idle hands to do. . . . The home seems to be disappearing, and crime, despite an increasingly effective police and probation system, is increasing everywhere."[19]

Another way of avoiding the idleness of the summer was to place children in vacation camps. One writer in the *Review of Reviews* in 1896 claimed that vacation camps for "tenement-house lads may well result more decisively in the formation of good character than all the school experiences of the rest of the year in town. . . ."[20] Vacation camps for tenement children received their initial spark from the establishment of a Fresh Air Fund in New York City. Jacob Riis reported that the idea got started when a young clergyman in Pennsylvania decided to bring tenement children from New York to live with members of his congregation. Riis wrote that the minister knew that "not for [the tenement children] was the robin's song they scarcely heard; not for them the summer fields or the cool forest shade, the sweet smell of briar and fern." The minister took to his home sixty children from the slums.[21] In 1882 the Tribune Newspaper promoted a Fresh Air Fund to help this enterprise. By 1891, 94,000 children were being placed in homes within a 500 mile radius of New York City. In 1890 William R. George, after being frustrated by his inability to place children in homes under the Fresh Air Fund, decided to establish a

camp. This camp, which eventually became a year round institution, was hailed as the "most attractive and promising experiment" in vacation camps and was visited and praised by all the
leading reformers in New York.[22]

William R. George was a successful New York businessman
who claimed that one summer while planning a vacation he
encountered a very moving newspaper story. The story dealt
with a little boy who thought he spied a daisy growing in the
New York Hall park. The little boy ran to pick it up only to
discover that it was a orange peel. The story concluded:
"Dear little boy, of such is life! The April sun is warm and just.
It shines alike on spring's flower, and on the bit of orange
peel!"[23] George wrote that he was so moved by the thought of
how many city children were missing the benefits of nature
that he canceled his vacation and contacted the Fresh Air
Fund. He wrote to his relatives in upstate New York to find
summer homes for urban youth. Being unable to find any
willing relatives George went ahead and established his own
Fresh Air Camp. By 1892 his Fresh Air Colony at Freeville,
New York, had five hundred summer residents.

George was never completely happy with the idea of just
giving his tenement charges a free vacation. He found that
natural surroundings were not enough to reform a character
shaped by the slums. His search for a method to provide
charity that did not corrupt led him to the idea of a Junior
Republic. In 1895 he organized his camp into a miniature
political and economic system. The Junior Republic manufactured its own money which was distributed in the form of pay
through various shops and projects run by the Republic. An
individual was paid on the basis of his ability to do a certain
task, such as carpentry or printing. A member of the Republic
was not required to work but if he were without enough
money to purchase lodgings within the Republic, he was ar-
rested for vagrancy and placed in the Republic jail. Prisoners
were put in steel cages and given bread and water to eat and
the job of crushing rocks. The citizens of the Republic were
required to purchase all of their necessities. These included
food, lodgings, and clothes. The quality of these items depended

upon what the citizens were able and willing to pay. If they had worked hard, they could afford to eat at the Republic's "Delmonico's" and rent a room at the "Waldorf" hotel. If they were poor workers or unwise in the use of their money, they would be forced to eat in a lower class restaurant and sleep in the attic dormitory. The hotels, restaurants, and stores were run by citizen entrepreneurs. The government of the Republic was organized around the idea of the town meeting with the junior citizens in control.[24]

What George had in mind when organizing his Republic was to create the conditions that existed before the city had triumphed in American life. He believed that the town meeting coupled with an economic system that provided for rapid mobility would recreate those conditions that had supposedly implanted virtue in the native American. One of George's favorite moral anecdotes dealt with a citizen who after several arrests for vagrancy was rehabilitated and began to practice the art of thrift. George reported that the boy told him, ". . . de odder weeks when I got me money I blowed it all in quick, so to-day when I got me cash, I made seven piles of it and in each I put enough money to carry me tru de day." George was not only happy that the boy was reformed but he also saw the boy carrying the influence of the Republic back into the urban environment. The boy told George, "I wuz thinking . . . how . . . we might do de same wid Pop's cash when we go back to de city. You see Pop don't get much money, but what he does get, we use most of it Saturday night when we go to de teater and gettin ice cream and candy and a lot of odder tings, and before de week is over we get hard up and have to ask de missionary lady or somebody else to helpt us out. . . ."[25]

A more practical way of channeling youthful activity into the right moral environment was the boys' club. Jacob Riis wrote that "it is by the boys' club that the street is hardest hit. In the fight for the lad it is that which knocks out the gang, and with its own weapon—the weapon of organization."[26] The first reported boys' club was established in New York in 1878. The principal object of the club was "to provide quiet and innocent amusement sufficiently attractive to draw the boys away from the danger of the street."[27] Clubs eventually became an integral part of the playground movement. When the field houses were constructed for the Chicago park system, they included facilities for club meetings. In 1892 Riis listed thirty-three boys' clubs in New York City.[28]

The emphasis on parks, recreation, and clubs to keep children off the city streets caused a major change in education. In a book published in 1910 on *Wider Use of the School Plant* the author began by noting, "The children who went to school back in the eighties skipped out of the school house door at half past three and scampered down the street shouting with glee. . . . Within a couple of decades all this has changed." Now he found that public school buildings were "open in some places every week-day in the year. They are open not only days but evenings. . . . Children go to them Saturdays as well as Mondays, and in some places the school rooms are not left unvisited even on Sundays."[29] The schools were the most logical institutions to assume the responsibility for controlling urban youth. Their buildings could be used after school hours and many of the activities could be incorporated into the school program.

These added educational duties were not always well received by the school people. Many of them felt that playgrounds and clubs had little to do with the purposes of education. There was also feeling against the idea of the school assuming control and direction over the social life of its students. One teacher in 1899 in a paper given before the Michigan Schoolmasters' Club argued, "There is no necessity for a high school in a city to take upon itself the establishing of social functions. Our greatest trouble is not in furnishing to our pupils sufficient social life, but in restraining them from the over abundant opportunities offered in the outside surroundings. . . ." The speaker went on to state her concern that the school, by involving itself in the social life of its students, was treading on dangerous ground. The school could never fully understand what it might accomplish by institutionalizing social relationships. "For my part," the speaker said, "I am unwilling thus to risk tangling the threads of fate."[30] Some school districts refused to get involved in these extra-curricular activities. A 1909 Leavenworth (Kansas) announcement stated, "The high school can take no responsibility for the social life of the students; this responsibility must be assumed by the home." The principal of the same school ten years later called this old-fashioned nonsense and argued that the school had to assume this responsibility. "With the replacing of such traditions as the woodpile and the dooryard pump in city homes by water and gas in the kitchen," wrote the principal, "has passed largely the boy's opportunity to form the habits of responsibility for contributing to the group."[31] A report by the principal of Central High School in Washington, D.C., in 1907 stated that there would be no school clubs. The principal wrote that "much more remains to be done in awakening parents to a realization of the danger to the pupil from all this scattering of his energies and in making them understand that because a club has a school name it is not necessarily a vital or necessary part of the school life."[32]

In New York the schools rapidly extended their control over the social life of students. Riis recalled that in 1895 the chairman of the Advisory Committee on Small Parks of New York City asked the police to indicate on a map the areas of high rates of juvenile delinquency. The committee found that all areas with newly founded parks had a decreasing rate, so it attempted to speed the development of parks by proposing a law which was eventually adopted. The law stated, "Hereafter no schoolhouse shall be constructed in the City of New York without an open-air playground attached to or used in connection with the same."[33] New York by 1910 was keeping its school playgrounds open under supervision after school hours and during the summer. The schools offered organized games, folk dancing, theatricals, and showers during the summer months.[34] In 1898 Wilson Gill, president of the American Patriotic League and member of the New York Reform Club, successfully petitioned the Boards of Education of Manhattan and the Bronx to allow the school buildings to remain open after hours. Gill was interested in organizing school clubs to channel youthful energies into patriotic activities. The boards granted his request and created a new position called the superintendent of clubs and recreations and opened the schools to after-school activities.[35] In 1903 New York City organized a Public Schools Athletic League to conduct athletic contests between New York schools. The organizer of the league and director of physical training in the New York schools was Dr. Luther Halsey Gulick. Gulick later became the first president of the Playground and Recreation Association and was one of the early leaders of the play movement which Curtis had described as being primarily concerned with using play to decrease juvenile delinquency. The first major athletic event sponsored by the league brought 1,500 boys together to compete at indoor sports at Madison Square Garden.[36]

These added school activities meant that teachers had to devote part of their school time to non-academic activities. Dr. Gulick wrote that the league would not have succeeded if it did not have the "continuous and enthusiastic support of principals and teachers. During the past year four hundred and eleven men have contributed their services toward helping their boys in athletics, during one or more hours per week after school hours." Gulick went on to give educational justification for this free use of the teacher's time by claiming that "this has resulted in that close alliance of teacher and pupil which is difficult to secure when the only relationship is that maintained during school hours."[37]

The expansion of school activities followed a similar pattern in other cities. In 1901 the Detroit Council of Women asked the city council for permission to conduct a playground on the site of an abandoned reservoir. When the council refused to give its permission, the women obtained use of a school yard and organized it into a playground. The following year the school board refused to grant a request for $1,200 for playground work in the city schools. The Council of Women then launched a successful campaign to convince the city and the school board of the necessity for adding playgrounds to the public school buildings. In Philadelphia school playgrounds were the result of a campaign conducted by the Civic Club. In 1894 the Civic Club held public meetings and presented petitions to the school board demanding public school playgrounds. The Philadelphia Board of Education opened four school playgrounds in 1895 and increased their number until by 1910 they had sixty-five playgrounds on school premises. In Boston, playgrounds were attached to school buildings after a Boston statistician computed that the usage of municipal playgrounds was limited to the radius of a six-mile walk. Since school buildings fell into this general pattern, it was considered more efficient and useful to attach the playgrounds to the school buildings.[38]

The opening of the school building after school hours eventually led to the establishment of evening recreation centers. These recreation centers offered club and athletic activities to both adults and children. Chicago opened two centers in 1909 which provided study facilities for students and organized athletics. In Chicago the centers meant an added responsibility for the regular school staff. The centers were put under the direction of the day-school principals and relied upon volunteer help. The evening centers in New York included not only athletics and clubs but also social dancing to draw people away from the commercial dancing halls. The leader of the centers in New York strongly emphasized their role in reducing urban crime. Her reports to the city superintendent of schools were full of anecdotes describing the conversion of city toughs into respectable citizens. In her 1906 report she described how the leader of one club of street loafers was changed from "a swaggering, unclean fellow" by the influence of "the athlete's code of honor." The code of honor, she wrote, "is a triumph over lawlessness, the beginning of a citizen's conception of duty." In 1908 it was claimed for the New York centers "the rescue of what the police designated 'one of the worst gangs of girls on the East Side.'"[39]

Sociologist Edward Ross in the late 1890's referred to the expansion of school activities as "an economical system of police," and placed it under his more general heading of social control.[40] The concept of social control was one that existed early in American education. The two major forms of social control were direct and indirect. The direct methods included the use of force and political techniques to maintain social order. The indirect methods of maintaining social order involved control of behavior through training and mental forms of persuasion. In a sense the American revolution replaced the use of force with education as a means of maintaining social order. There was a strong feeling that some method had to be used to assure good character otherwise a Republican government would result in social chaos. This was one reason why the Northwest Ordinance in 1787 set aside land for education. The ordinance stated, "Religion, morality, and knowledge, being necessary to good government and the happiness of mankind, schools and the means of education shall forever be encouraged." The same sentiment was expressed in the 1789 Massachusetts law establishing school districts. The law stated that it would be the duty of all colleges, academies, and schools in Massachusetts "to impress on the minds of children and youth . . . love of their country, humanity, and universal benevolence; sobriety, industry, and frugality; chastity, moderation, and temperance; . . . to lead . . . into a clear understanding of the tendency of the above-mentioned virtues to preserve and perfect a republican Constitution and secure the blessings of liberty. . . ."41

The idea of education as an inexpensive form of police was part of Horace Mann's argument for the common school in the 1830's and 1840's. Mann argued in an 1848 report to the Massachusetts State Board of Education that all forms of controlling human action, except education, had failed. He wrote that "all means and laws designed to repress injustice and crime, give occasion to new injustice and crime. For every lock that is made, a false key is made to pick it; and for every Paradise that is created, there is a Satan who would scale its walls. . . ." The one experiment he suggested that had never been tried was the ending of immorality through a universal system of education. Through the shaping of character in the schools an entire reform of society could be accomplished. "In all attempts to reform mankind," he told the state board, ". . . whether by changing the frame of government, by aggravating or softening the severity of the penal code . . . in all these attempts, the infantile and youthful mind, its amenability to influence, and the enduring and self-operating character of the influences it receives, have been almost wholly unrecognized."[42]

The expansion of school activities was therefore a continuation of traditional attitudes regarding the social role of education. It implemented the social control aspect of education by providing greater organizational methods. More and more children spent more and more time in some form of school activity. One effect of the growth of the school might have been to undermine the social training capabilities of the home and church. A common argument during the period was that the family and church were collapsing and therefore the schools had to fill the void. Whether this was true or not is difficult to measure, but it does suggest that many educators viewed themselves as assuming a dominant position in the social and moral training of the child.

II

Education responded to what was perceived to be the disintegration of human relationships in the growing urban areas by attempting to use the schools as a new focal point for community life. The image of the city was similar to the one applied to other corporate bodies. Specialization and the interdependence of the city required both a cooperative individualism and a coordination of individual tasks. Herbert Croly's concern with establishing a set of common allegiances that would transcend purely individualistic economic motives was widely shared by Americans who believed the city was destroying the traditional community of close interpersonal relationships. Urban Americans of the late nineteenth century tended nostalgically to view the past as one of small towns where a feeling of community resulted from face-to-face relationships making the individual aware of the interdependence of people and a common set of mutual interests. The city through its size and impersonality made man a cipher in a crowd without any consciousness of a shared set of interests. It was believed the lack of a sense of community in the city was contributing to class antagonisms, the deterioration of municipal politics, and the psychological instability of the urban man.

The use of the school as a social center was thought of as one means of re-establishing within the urban context a new sense of community. The neighborhood school would be the vehicle for organizing the city into a corporate body of specialized tasks and life styles cemented together by common allegiances. An example of this attitude was a New York writer who in 1898 argued that democracy could only function with the spirit of a democratic fraternalism resulting from the unification of individual aspirations into a common way of life. "It is just this [the common life]," he claimed, "that we of this crowded, busy nineteenth-century metropolis are most deficient. . . ." He argued that the school by opening its doors a little wider could bring in neighborhood lift and create the spirit of democratic fraternalism by becoming a social center.[43] An article in the *Atlantic Monthly* in 1896 suggested the school could attract more people by improving the beauty of its buildings, by attaching a public library, by organizing a museum and conservatory, and by using its walls as a public art gallery. The author wrote, "The common schoolhouse is in reality the most obvious centre of national unity. . . ." The school in this case would function as a center to organize neighborhood, city, and national unity.[44]

In 1902 John Dewey brought the social center idea to the National Education Association convention. He told the gathered educators that the schools must provide a "means for bringing people and their ideas and beliefs together, in such ways as will lessen friction and instability, and introduce deeper sympathy and wider understanding." Using the schools as social centers, he believed, could morally uplift the quality of urban living by replacing brothels, saloons, and dance halls as centers of recreation. More importantly he saw the social center as a social clearing house of ideas that would interpret to the urban industrial worker the meaning of his place in the modern world. Through an exchange of ideas and the establishment of relationships with a variety of people there would develop an understanding of others and the mutual bonds of an interdependent society. The social center, Dewey told his audience, "must interpret to [the worker] the intellectual and social meaning of the work in which he is engaged; that is, must reveal its relations to the life and work of the world." For Dewey the school as a social center would be instrumental in bringing about the national form of allegiance sought by Croly.[45]

During the 1890's the social centers developed rapidly throughout the country. In 1897 New York organized its after school recreational activities into social centers. The University Settlement in New York organized clubs in twenty-one school buildings for the specific purpose of reducing individual selfishness and promoting a spirit of social cooperation.[46] In Chicago the social centers were established in the fieldhouses of the park systems with neighborhood groups engaged in a variety of activities including community orchestras and choral clubs.[47] A local women's club in Milwaukee persuaded the city in 1907 to open school buildings for local evening meetings.[48] When the Russell Sage Foundation surveyed the social center movement in 1913, it found of 788 school superintendents contacted around the country, 330 reported the use of their school as social centers. By 1920 the movement had spread to 667 school districts.[49]

Changes in school architecture reflected the growing commitment to the social center idea. One school superintendent complained to his colleagues in 1897 that it was difficult opening schools to adults because in most buildings access to assembly rooms was "gained only by climbing flights of stairs, always with embarrassment and often with risk of accident from fire or other causes." His suggestion, which appears to have been incorporated in future school plans, was to construct the assembly rooms on the ground floor with easy access from the street.[50] Classroom furniture also had to be changed for the multiple use of school and adult social center. Demands were made for the replacement of the school desks bolted to the floor with flat-top desks that could be rearranged and utilized for club and recreational activities. By 1910 schools such as the

Washington Irving High School in New York were being specifically designed to function as social centers. The lobby of the Washington Irving High School contained a neighborhood art gallery and the auditorium was designed to provide facilities for neighborhood drama groups. Office space was set aside in the school to accommodate the staffs of local clubs and associations. The adult night school was organized so that the worker's life might flow evenly between the job and school. Students could come directly from their places of work, "have supper in the lunch rooms, recreation in the gymnasium, and take up their studies with refreshed minds and bodies."[51]

One important ingredient in the social center movement, besides the emphasis upon unity and cooperation, was teaching the immigrant how to adjust to urban living. For instance, the Women's Municipal League of Boston worked for the opening of social centers in the local schools as part of their more general civic work directed at improving the lives of immigrants. The president of the league wrote in 1912 that social centers were opened because "it is our endeavor to make our city a true home for the people, it is not enough that we should merely make it a house. . . . We must also ensure that there shall be within it recreation, enjoyment, and happiness for all." The league's work in helping to make Boston a home included the establishment of a Fly and Milk Committee and the inspection of local markets and streets. The league organized a traveling exhibit that displayed to Bostonians pictures of clean and dirty alleys, a life-sized model of a dirty market with actual displays of dirty food, and models of sanitary and unsanitary tenement buildings. The social centers organized by the league in one high school provided "educational recreation" and fourteen clubs called the East Opportunity Clubs.[52]

It was believed that building community cooperation depended on breaking down barriers between religion, caste, and political partisanship. In 1909 *Survey* published an article by social center organizer Edward J. Ward in which one of the two accompanying cartoons depicted members of the Progressive, Socialist, Republican, and Democratic parties running into an elevator to escape a storm of prejudice and misunderstanding. The elevator was marked civic club, and it was preparing to take the escaping political members up to a brightly lit school center with municipal improvement posters on its bulletin boards. The other cartoon showed happy singing coming from behind the door of a civic club in a school social center. Outside the door of the club were hung coats with the names of all the major religions on them and against the wall were placed the banners of the four political parties. The author of the article claimed as ancestor to the school social center the "Little Red School House" which in a previous age had combated the elements of community dissension by providing a common meeting place.[53]

Edward J. Ward first launched his campaign for school social centers in Rochester, New York, in 1907 as a means of reforming urban politics. Ward advocated throughout the country the establishment of social centers in schoolhouses as centers for political discussion. He envisioned the day when the voting districts would be the same as the school districts and the ballot box would be placed in the schoolhouse. "When the ballot box is placed in the schoolhouse," he wrote, "this building becomes, for all its possible wider uses, the real social center; and the way is clear and the means are at hand for supplying the fundamental and supreme lack in the machinery of democracy."[54] Ward's advocacy of political social centers must be placed in the context of the general development of civic clubs throughout the country. A book entitled *Municipal Reform Movements in the United States,* published in 1895, listed the development in the United States of fifty-seven civic and municipal clubs, thirteen municipal betterment groups, and eight women's reform organizations. Like Ward's social center the majority of these groups defined as their purpose the establishment of a non-partisan political organization. Typical of these groups was the Citizens' Association of Albany whose goal was the promotion of "the interest of neither political party, but [who] expects to convince both parties that when dishonest and corrupt men are nominated for office citizens will . . . not . . . vote . . . for them, and to warn those who seek office simply for the purpose of plundering the public treasury that their malfeasance in office will be exposed. . . ." The civic club was essentially another political organization for those who found they could not work through existing party machinery. Their targets were the local ward bosses who exercised great power because of the support of their constituencies. The civic clubs sought to undermine this support by attracting the electorate into a non-partisan political group. This was one major reason for the emphasis by many reform groups on prohibition. For instance, the Citizen's League of Norwalk, Connecticut, defined as its major object the destruction of the saloon because it was "believed to be the center of vice, crime, and corruption in politics." Translated this meant voters who exercised political influence on the boss were the working men who frequented the saloons, and removing politics from the saloon meant bringing it under the influence of the Citizen's League.[55]

Indicative of how closely Ward's social centers paralleled the work of civic reform clubs was the opposition to the social center movement shown by the local political boss of Rochester, George W. Aldridge. In the words of magazine writer, Ray Stannard Baker, Aldridge attacked the social centers in 1910 because "the truth was getting out! And from the schools the reports of the discussions were getting into the newspapers."[56] Aldridge quite naturally became a victim of the social center because it was precisely the people who felt they could not express themselves through the existing political structure who were attracted to the school meetings. When the Rochester School Board granted the use of three buildings in 1907, Ward called them a new form of "neighborhood political discussion headquarters." The preamble to the constitution of Rochester's first social center stated as its object "the gaining of information upon public questions by listening to public speakers and by public readings and discussions."[57] When Aldridge was defeated in 1910, Baker claimed it was the result of a revitalized Chamber of Commerce and the "truth" that came forth from the free civic discussions of the social centers.[58]

Of course, it was not Ward's intention to make social centers into exclusive civic reform clubs, nor was there any evidence that this was advocated by other groups. What existed was a basic belief that if the people were brought together, the better elements of the community would assume leadership. It was assumed the leadership would be taken over by the expert who would guide the cooperatively organized electorate into making decisions related to mutual interests. The divisiveness of party politics would be replaced by a spirit of democratic fraternalism working for the betterment of the whole community. The writer of *Municipal Reform Movements in the United States* remarked "that the masses do not lead in any great reform. . . . Men crave leaders, and instinctively look up to those who will guide them under inspiration of a great cause. . . ."[59] This was the theory of a democratic elite that Ward incorporated into his idea of social centers. In reference to Hamilton's description of the people as a great beast, Ward wrote, "The people, the organized body of the citizenship has a unity, a selfhood, but it is no more conscious of it than are the coordinated cells of a cabbage leaf of their unity. The people is not a great beast. The people is a great vegetable."[60] For Ward, Croly's "new nationalism" would be the result of the schoolhouse used for the town meeting.

Of the 667 school districts that reported social centers to the Russell Sage Foundation in 1920 it is difficult to determine how many acted as just neighborhood social and recreational centers, or how many followed the more political designs of Rochester's social centers. Ward did organize a National Conference of Civic and Social Center Development which met in Madison, Wisconsin, in 1911 and brought together 200 delegates. The conference was addressed by six mayors and three governors, including Woodrow Wilson, who at that time was governor of New Jersey. Wilson reminded the gathered delegates of the strong reformist movement started in Rochester by the social centers. "The minute they began talking," Wilson said, ". . . it became impossible for those scores of things in our politics that will stop the moment they are mentioned on the street corners . . . treatment for bad politics is exactly the modern treatment for tuberculosis—exposure to the open air." Wilson emphasized the role of school centers in promoting class unity and in ending social class conflict when he likened the

American community to a human body and told the people in Madison, "There can be no real life in a community so long as its parts are segregated and separated; it is just as if you separated the organs of the human body and then expected them to produce life. . . ."[61]

As the school social center idea spread throughout the United States it took on a variety of forms. In Chicago the park field houses served the function of bringing the community together on a social basis, while the schoolhouses were used to promote political cooperation. In 1914 the Russell Sage Foundation reported that 142 political meetings had been held in Chicago school buildings during a municipal election. The Chicago Board of Education proudly announced that "in no case was it necessary to require the forfeiture of the $25 deposit because of damage or infraction of the rules of the board." The civic clubs of Los Angeles fought to have the polling booths and political meetings in school buildings. This had been Ward's dream of uniting politics and community. The civic club leaders in Los Angeles wanted the use of public school buildings "instead of livery stables and small, dingy, out-of-the-way and hard-to-find places." The argument was given that under the old plan no one knew where the polling booths would be located except the machine.[62] It was also argued in many cities that with the growing extension of women's suffrage, a clean decent place, like a schoolhouse, should be used for political purposes.

The main emphasis of the arguments supporting the use of schoolhouses for political cooperation continued to be to destroy boss rule. Clarence A. Perry, the Russell Sage Foundation expert on social centers and author of innumerable tracts on the topic, wrote in 1914, "In the political world the continually repeated spectacle of corrupt boss control is causing widespread appreciation of the need of meeting-places which will invite a loftier and more general discussion of platforms. . . ." Perry suggested that social center functions could be divided between the elementary and secondary schools. The elementary schools could serve neighborhood organizations and the high school could be used for functions that involved a large area of the city. Perry wanted not only non-partisan discussions and the ballot box in the school, but also party rallies and primaries.[63] Another wide-ranging vision of the future use of the schoolhouse was made by Frank Walsh, chairman of the National Commission on Industrial Relations, at a social center week held at Chautauqua in 1913. Walsh expressed his opinion at the Chautauqua meeting that the splintering of the Republican party in 1912 sounded the death knell to party conventions. He now felt it was up to the schools, acting as social centers, to fill the vacuum caused by the passing of the national convention system.[64]

The impact of the schools as centers for political unity and civic cooperation was considerably reduced during this period by their steady withdrawal from community influence. The professionalization of educational expertise and the reorganization of urban school systems tended to undercut efforts to make the school the center of community life. While the schools expanded their activities to all sectors of life, the actual control of educational systems became increasingly centralized and bureaucratic. Like other organizations in the United States education adopted the corporate image as a model for both the administration of the individual school and the coordination of the parts of school systems. While efficiency of operation was often given as a reason for these changes, there did exist a strong nativist sentiment that saw this as an opportunity to remove control of the schools from the hands of Catholics and immigrants. The result was to doom completely all attempts to make the school the true community center.

The withdrawal of community control of the schools occurred with the reform of municipal politics in the late nineteenth and early twentieth centuries. The great enemy of the political reformer was the ward boss whose activities it was believed centered around graft and the buying of votes in neighborhood saloons. In many cases municipal reformers combined the prohibition issue with the destruction of the power of ward bosses. It was believed the end of the saloon would mean the end of the center of corrupt political activities. Graft and corruption were, of course, involved in the ward system, but the ward boss also took a great deal of responsibility for his constituents. In many cases the local ward leader provided important social services to the people in his neighborhood that were unavailable through any other means. The ward boss did have to be elected and was therefore susceptible to local community pressures.

What the destruction of the ward system meant for both the schools and the municipal government was a decrease in local community power within the city. Municipal reformers usually sought as a replacement for the ward system city councils that were elected on a city wide basis. The result of this change is shown in the example of Pittsburgh which in 1911 switched from a ward system to city wide election of nine city council members and fifteen school board members. The previous ward systems had 387 elected officials. Immediately prior to the change in government organization the majority (67%) of the elected officials under the ward system were "small business-men—grocers, saloonkeepers, livery-stable proprietors, owners of small hotels, druggists—white-collar workers such as clerks and bookkeepers, and skilled and unskilled workmen." Under the new system the 1911 election produced no council members who were small businessmen or white-collar workers. Each body contained only one person that might be called a rep-resentative of the working class.[65] Not only was community control destroyed but representation from all social and eco-nomic classes was limited.

The attitude prevalent among reform groups with regard to control of the schools was made evident in a pamphlet published by the Voter's League of Pittsburgh during the 1911 election. The pamphlet deplored the fact that school boards contained only a small number of "men prominent throughout the city in business life . . . in professional occupations . . . holding positions as managers, secretaries, auditors, superinten-dents and foremen." It was argued that a man's occupation was a strong indication of his qualifications for the school board. "Employment as ordinary laborer and in the lowest class of mill work would naturally lead to the conclusion that such men did not have sufficient education or business training to act as school directors." Included was a list of those it felt should not be on school boards, "small shopkeepers, clerks, workmen at any trades, who by lack of educational advantages and business training, could not, no matter how honest, be expected to administer properly the affairs of an educational system."[66]

Similar patterns of shifting control occurred in other cities. Sol Cohen has shown that reform movements in New York City combined destruction of ward control of the schools with anti-Catholic sentiments. In the 1894 New York election a reform mayor was elected who fought for the centralization of control of the schools and their removal from politics. Under the traditional New York ward system the mayor appointed twenty-one commissioners of common schools and they in turn appointed five trustees for each ward. The ward trustees appointed all teachers and janitors, nominated principals and vice-principals, and furnished school supplies. This system, of course, provided opportunity for graft but it also created a situation where the trustee had to be sensitive to local needs and desires. Sol Cohen states, "The reformers' battle cry, 'Take the school out of politics,' not only meant take the schools out of the hands of Tammany Hall it also meant take the schools out of the hands of the Roman Catholic Church."[67]

Accompanying the declining local control of the schools was the increasing bureaucratization of urban educational systems. Role differentiation, specialization, and centralization of school administration all contributed to a decrease in lay influence on the schools. To a great extent this was the result of the desire by educators to protect themselves professionally and the need for rationally organized plans to govern large school districts. One of the major steps toward centralization was concentrating the governing power of the school system in the office of superintendent. This relocation of power did not occur without some protest. One writer in the *Atlantic* in 1896 complained that in many areas the idea of a school superintendent was "opposed, and it continues to be opposed . . . because it seems to withdraw the schools from immediate contact with the people as represented by their elected school committee." The writer dismissed this argument on the grounds that as society grew more complex democratic management of affairs had to yield to "republican methods."[68] Eventually the superintendent's authority in most school systems was given legal sanction. In Boston, for example, the school committee in 1884 passed this regulation: "The superintendent shall be responsible to the school board as the executive in the department of instruction over all supervisors, principals, and other instructors."[69]

The rise of an urban educational bureaucracy has been the subject of an excellent study by Michael B. Katz.[70] Katz has shown that in the case of Boston a well-defined and full-scale bureaucracy emerged between 1850 and 1876. Using Carl Freidrich's definition, Katz lists the elements of a bureaucracy as the "centralization of control and supervision, differentiation of function . . . qualification for office . . . rules defining desirable habit or behavior patterns of all members of such an organization, namely, objectivity, precision and consistency, and discretion." These, of course, were all organizational developments that eventually became inflexible and remote from outside pressures. The results were not surprising since they represented the very forces that structured bureaucratic organizations. In the case of Boston, Katz found that the reasons for the development of a bureaucracy were "the increasing complexity of urban school administration, the interference of politics and personalistic motives with school operation, the apparently successful example of industry in solving the problems involved in managing and coordinating large numbers of people and, finally, the aspirations and anxieties of schoolmen themselves." Rigid organization and centralization of power freed the schools from political and personal interference at the expense of sensitivity to community pressures. Protective organizational measures clearly defined the roles, qualifications, and procedures for promotion of teachers and at the same time shielded them from the people in the particular area where they were assigned to teach.

As in other urban areas centralization of the control of Boston schools revealed undercurrents of strong anti-immigrant attitudes. In 1875 leaders of the Boston community attacked the school system for being too rigid and costly. One of their first achievements was a bill passed by the state legislature that reduced school board membership from one hundred and eighteen members elected from wards to twenty-four elected on a citywide basis. Michael Katz reports strong Catholic opposition to the bill because it excluded them from management of the schools. This situation was similar to the one Sol Cohen found in New York in the 1890's. *The Boston Pilot* was quite explicit about what it thought were the underlying motives for the changes in school board organization. The editor of the *Pilot* stated "he was told by members of the Legislature, that the committee that framed the Bill had asked several members of the House and Senate to support it because 'it would exclude the foreign elements from the School Board.' "[71]

The hard shell of bureaucracy provided protection for school systems that were basically hostile to their environments and to large numbers of the people they served. The Black Revolution of the nineteen fifties and sixties clearly exposed the degree to which urban schools had become unresponsive to the needs of the community. It was only through demonstrations, violence, and strong political pressures that the Black population was able to gain improvements and changes. Extreme measures were used because all other channels of influence had been effectively closed by previous school reforms. The removal of the urban school from politics left the Black man with no other choice except the tactics of confrontation. Only through the use of these techniques could he gain access to the instruments of power. Confrontation established lines of communication where none had previously existed and proved effective in cutting through the protective shell of bureaucratic procedure.

Professionalized and bureaucratic control of education became a barrier to establishing the school as a meaningful center or community life in the city. Schools were instruments for shaping community life along lines determined by the expertise of the organizer. Since the community lacked direct channels of influence on the schools, the social centers never became an expression of neighborhood life but functioned rather to impose a concept of organization on the community. As has been noted earlier, the leaders of the social center movement tempered their idea of democratic fraternalism with elitist concepts. The social centers were to organize the community into a corporate body that followed "right-minded" leadership. While it is impossible to determine the extent to which this lessened the impact of the social center movement on urban life, it can be argued that the interests of the community were not always the interests of the social center organizer and, consequently, the establishment of democratic fraternalism was not in all cases possible. The school as a social center might have worked if its organization and control had come directly from the community. This, of course, became impossible as the channels of public influence on the schools were slowly closed.

CHAPTER FIVE

VOCATIONAL GUIDANCE, THE JUNIOR HIGH SCHOOL, AND ADOLESCENCE

The first decade of the twentieth century witnessed the full-fledged birth of two new educational institutions, vocational guidance and the junior high school. Both of these movements grew in response to the specialized needs of the new corporate society. The early vocational guidance leaders attempted to function as human engineers who shaped individual abilities to fit a particular slot in the social organism. This gave them the dual responsibility of analyzing personal talents and character and planning educational programs in terms of a future vocation. Junior high schools were designed to make educational planning and guidance possible at an early age. The original purpose of the junior high school was to differentiate students into separate courses of study according to abilities and vocational goals. It was hoped that with proper guidance the student would choose a vocation in the junior high and then follow an educational program through the high school directly to the occupation.

There was something of an engineer's image of social organization about the idea of education functioning as a feeder system to the industrial complex. Certainly there was an element of frustration among early vocational guidance leaders about the instability of human beings keeping society from functioning like a well-oiled machine. Frank Parsons, often called the father of vocational guidance and founder of the first vocational bureau in Boston in 1908, wrote that a "sensible industrial system will . . . seek . . . to put men, as well as timber, stone, and iron, in the places for which their natures fit them, and to polish and prepare them for efficient service with at least as much care as is bestowed upon clocks, electric dynamos or locomotives."[1] This language reflected Parsons' own training in engineering and his involvement in economic and social reform in the 1890's. A similar anxiety about human inefficiency permeated the work of pioneer industrial psychologist, Hugo Munsterberg. Munsterberg provided the early guidance movement with vocational aptitude tests. In a book published in 1910 he complained about the lack of social barriers and economic conditions that allowed men to drift into careers for which they were not suited. In the past America "could afford the limitless waste of human energy just as it felt justified in wasting the timber resources of the forest."[2] Modern conditions, Munsterberg felt, required both the conservation of resources and human talents. The specialized conditions of society could not afford the social and economic waste caused by having the wrong man perform an economic or political task.

Vocational guidance was to reduce the inefficiency of the distribution of human resources. One example was Eli Weaver, the pioneer of vocational guidance in New York City, who envisioned the establishment of a central government vocational bureau that would function as a commodity exchange market. He made this proposal after organizing between 1906 and 1910 committees of teachers in the New York high schools to work with students in planning their careers. The function of the central bureau would be to determine the type of training and character needed in available industrial occupations. The bureau would also conduct surveys of the labor market to determine manpower shortages and surpluses. This information was to be used to encourage and discourage training in particular occupations depending upon the needs of the labor market. Within the schools guidance and educational programs were to be based on information supplied by the bureau. The bureau also was to place the graduates in appropriate occupations. Weaver wrote that the guidance agency would "facilitate the exchange of labor between the workers and employers as the exchange of other commodities is now assisted through the standardizing operations of other exchanges."[3]

Vocational guidance was also conceived of as a means of changing the general pattern of industrial development. One way was to keep workers out of certain types of industry. J. Adams Puffer, the principal of the Lyman School for Boys and director of the Beacon Vocation Bureau in Boston, argued in a book published in 1913 that vocational guidance should channel youth into constructive and not neutral or destructive occupations. Puffer labeled as destructive, liquor, patent medicines, unwholesome foods, vicious amusements, and commercial pirates. Neutral occupations were harmless but non-contributive to the efficiency of the social order. Puffer wrote, "If each teacher in the United States, each year, guided into constructive work one single boy or girl who would otherwise have followed some neutral or destructive occupation, that alone would probably wipe out the whole of both non-constructive groups."[4]

Frank Parsons was another example. He was a utopian reformer who believed that vocational guidance was one step in the direction of eliminating the profit motive from the industrial system. Parsons opened the Vocation Bureau in Boston in the last year of a life that had been devoted to campaigns for social and economic change. A hope he once expressed was that some day "the humblest student of social science may drop some word, that, taking root in the brain of a man who trundles the world at his heels, shall lift the earth into Paradise."[5] The paradise that Parsons was hoping for was called "mutualism." This was a blissful state of brotherly love in which conflict and antagonism were replaced by mutual help. He believed that mutualism could only be achieved through the gradual expansion of public ownership of the means of production. To achieve this required education and industrial efficiency. Industrial efficiency made it possible to run large corporate structures under public ownership, and education would "squeeze the last black drop of savage blood out of humanity's veins."[6]

Parson's ideas reflected how much vocational guidance was a response to the organizational revolution. He wrote in his book on mutualism, "Educate! Fill the children with public spirit. Enlarge the business interests of city, state, and nation. Make the railroads, monopolies, and trusts public property. . . . Educate! Educate! Teach brother-love, and practice it occasionally." Guidance into the corporate structure was one form of education designed to make the economic system run efficiently for the benefit of all. But vocational guidance was only part of a general educational plan to turn society into one large corporation of brotherly love. Another part of the plan was the creation of a guaranteed annual income that would condition men to think in terms of working for the good of society. External restraints on evil activities, such as saloons, and generous rewards for social service were to lead to internalization of these controls. The result was to be a highly organized society in which the individual was willing to sacrifice himself for the benefit of his neighbor. Performance of a job for which the individual was best suited was one way of fulfilling a social obligation. The individual in a state of mutualism, Parsons wrote, will work to the best of his abilities and without controls will consume "no more than he needs to fit him for the highest and noblest activities of which he is capable."[7]

The role of the vocational guidance counselor as it emerged from these more general social goals was part labor specialist, educator, and psychologist. As labor specialist the guidance counselor had to have an understanding of the job market and requirements. At the founding meeting of the Vocational Education Association in 1913 Frederick G. Bonser of Teachers College demanded that a professional education be developed that would train the vocational counselor to know the "relationship between present and probable supply and demand, the relative wages, and the changes in methods, devices, and organization effecting the workers. . . ." Bonser also emphasized the importance of studying the physical and mental requirements of occupations.[8]

There was a tendency in the early stages of the guidance movement to view the client as raw material for the industrial machine. Part of the educational duties of the counselor was that of shaping good industrial character. Parsons wrote, "Life can be moulded into any conceivable form. Draw up your specifications for a dog, or man . . . and if you will give me control of the environment, and time enough, I will clothe your dreams in flesh and blood."[9] In part this meant just the inculcation of traditional business values such as industriousness, punctuality, obedience, and orderliness. For example, as part of the guidance program at the De Kalb Township High School in Illinois the principal would quote business maxims such as, "It is none of my business what you do at night, but if dissipation affects what you do the next day, and you do half as much as I demand, you will last half as long as you hoped."[10] At the vocation bureau in Boston Parsons would use an interview and self-analysis sheet to determine what personality adjustments would be necessary for his clients. During the course of an interview Parsons would make his own character appraisal by watching the manners and habits of his subject. This appraisal would be followed by a take-home questionnaire. The instructions on the questionnaire told the client to, "Look in the glass. Watch yourself. Get your friends to . . . tell you confidentially what they think of your appearance, manners, voice. . . . Get your family and friends to help you recognize your defects. . . ." With these instructions the individual would answer questions ranging from self-reliance and industriousness to "do you wear your finger-nails in mourning and your linen overtime?"[11]

As a psychologist the early guidance counselor used a variety of tests to determine occupational abilities. The early tests developed by Munsterberg were designed to determine which Boston streetcar motormen would be least likely to have accidents. The tests could be generally described as comparing human abilities to a machine. Historically Munsterberg believed that he was bringing together two major movements in

American life, scientific management and vocational guidance. Scientific management, Munsterberg wrote in one of his major works in 1913, *Psychology and Industrial Efficiency,* had under the direction of the efficiency expert, Frederick Taylor, for example, made major advances in increasing industrial productivity. But, he argued, while the time-study approach did show how to increase the efficiency of a particular task, it did not go far enough in analyzing the physical traits best suited for the job. Working from the frame of reference of scientific management Munsterberg essentially tried to analyze the mechanical response of man. Taylor had wanted to mechanize human action with time and motion studies. Munsterberg wanted to determine how far and in what direction any given individual could be mechanized. His tests of Boston streetcar motormen were to determine powers of sustained attention and discrimination with respect to a rapidly changing panorama. The objective was to find those who would be least likely to have an accident. Working later with the American Telephone and Telegraph Company, Munsterberg developed tests of memory, attention, and dexterity for job applicants.[12] Tests of this nature were quickly used in guidance. For instance, Jesse B. Davis, a high school principal in Michigan and early vocational guidance leader, inspired by Hugo Munsterberg's streetcar and telephone tests, worked with the Michigan State Telephone Company in 1912 and 1913 to develop aptitude tests for telephone operators. These tests included the ability to remember numbers, speed, and motor accuracy.[13]

In the schools vocational guidance acquired the role of educational guidance and evaluator of individual interests and abilities. One school that became an early model for vocational guidance was the Grand Rapids Central School in Grand Rapids, Michigan. Its fame among guidance leaders was attested to by the fact that the first meeting of the Vocational Guidance Association was held in 1913 in Grand Rapids and the principal of the school, Jesse B. Davis, was elected the first secretary of the association. The following year Davis became its president.

Davis not only believed that the major function of the school was to guide the student into his proper place in the corporate structure but also that the school should be organized along the lines of a corporation. He believed that this would give the student a good introduction into the workings of the industrial community. The whole social life of the Central High School was organized to train the students for a corporate structure. Student groups were organized into a pyramid of activities. At the base were clubs, athletics, and student govern- ment. Above these activities in ascending order were a Boys and Girls Leadership Club, a Student Council, an Advisory Council, and the principal. Davis, the principal and founder of the system, believed that organization of all school activities into a social whole would demonstrate to the students the value of system and combination of effort. This type of organization he felt reflected the realities of an organized industrial system. He compared his position as principal to that of a general manager and called the advisory council of teachers, a board of control. Davis stated that "the ideals upon which honest living and sound business stand, are the ideals of the public schools." While these industrial traits were being learned in the social life of the school, class work was aiding the student to choose a job. Topics in English composition were assigned in progressive steps to help the individual understand himself and the type of career he should follow. In the ninth grade students at the high school analyzed their own character and habits. In the eleventh grade they chose a career and investigated the type of preparation they would need. In the twelfth grade the students made "a special study of the vocation with respect to its social obligations, its peculiar opportunities for human service, and responsibilities . . . [to] the community." Davis believed that people should enter an occupation with the idea that "it was the best means by which, they, with their ability, might serve their fellow man." This belief he placed in the historical context of the development of social interdependence.[14]

More typical of the developing role of the counselor was that suggested by Frank Parsons' successor as director of the Boston Vocation Bureau, Meyer Bloomfield. In an article in Charles Johnston's 1914 anthology, *The Modern High School,* he stated that the "vocational-guidance movement has . . .

made clear one of the most important and generally neglected services which a school can render, and that is educational guidance."[15] Educational guidance involved helping the student select an educational program to match his interests, abilities, and future occupation. The tools of the counselor were aptitude tests similar to those being developed by Munsterberg, interest inventories, and character analysis. An important requirement of educational guidance was a flexible curriculum. In terms of vocational guidance the curriculum was to be subservient to the occupational goals of the student. On one hand this meant evaluating subjects in terms of their vocational value. Bloomfield reported that this was occurring in several cities. "Such adjustments," he wrote, "and such reinterpretations of the high school scheme make for a fresh sense of values in secondary education."[16] On the other hand this meant having a differentiated curriculum. Students would take different courses of study depending on their occupational destination. Ideally the school counselor would match the student to an occupation and then to a course of study that would prepare him for that vocation.

The main argument for the junior high school was that it facilitated the differentiation and guidance of students. As Edward Krug has stated in his book, *The Shaping of the American High School,* the junior high school "put forward as advantageous features . . . the advancement of practical subjects, the provision for early differentiation, and the fostering of socialized aims."[17] For instance, a survey of New York junior high schools conducted between 1911 and 1913 listed as opportunities offered by the junior high: "(a) an opportunity to offer different courses of study; (b) an opportunity to adapt the instruction to the two sexes and to the requirements of high schools and vocational schools; (c) an opportunity to classify pupils according to ability."[18] The report appeared at a time when the New York schools were considering expanding their intermediate schools or junior highs from including just the seventh and eighth grades to inclusion of the ninth grade. New York had established its first seventh and eighth grade intermediate schools in 1905 and began adding the ninth grade in 1915.

Differentiation of the curriculum was also one of the major features of the first junior high to receive national attention in 1910. Superintendent Frank Bunker of the Berkeley, California school system wrote in support of his nationally publicized three year intermediate school, "To force all children in the seventh and eighth grades . . . to take the same work is clearly wrong."[19]

Guidance personnel had the key role of aiding the seventh and eighth grade student to choose a course of study from the differentiated curriculum. A report on the Rochester junior high schools stated that they provided "vocational counselors, teachers with shortened teaching programs, [who] confer with pupils and visit homes to consult with parents."[20] In other school systems the principal often functioned as counselor. For instance, the Los Angeles public schools opened its first junior high in 1911 with six courses of studies. The pupils made a choice between these six programs in the eighth grade with the aid of the principal. When San Francisco opened its first junior high in 1921, it stated as its preference for guidance, experience in various short courses.[21]

Another response to the guidance problem was the advisory or homeroom period. This special period was eventually utilized as both a center for social activity in the school and as part of the guidance program. One highly publicized example was the Ben Blewett School in St. Louis, Missouri. Beginning in the seventh grade each child at the Ben Blewett School spent 150 to 200 hours in advisory periods. During the course of the seventh grade, the student in the advisory period made a choice of a future career. In the eighth grade students were programmed into three different courses of study depending on their vocational choice. Principal Cox, organizer of the school in 1917, stated that a guiding principle was the "responsibility to each child as an individual, and to society, whose agent it is for leading the children as individuals and as groups toward the goal of social efficiency." Ben Blewett School also had a unique system of social tracking to help achieve this goal. Students in each course of study were tracked according to intellectual ability. To avoid the loss of social cohesion and training caused by differentiation and ability tracking, the school established "m,n,o groupings" which were "intended primarily to bring about, in social activities, cross sections of the other two types of groupings." It was claimed that in actual practice they were superfluous because "spontaneous and natural association of playground and extra-curricular activities apparently break indiscriminately across intellectual and vocational groupings."[22]

Both vocational guidance and the junior high school were based on the assumption that interests, abilities, and aptitudes stabilized and became fixed during the adolescent period. Meyer Bloomfield of the Boston Vocation Bureau reflected a rather pervasive view when he wrote, "Adolescence is the period of decisive battles, the time when the history of many an individual is almost finally written."[23] In a book of readings on vocational guidance published in 1915 Bloomfield offered as proof an article by Edward Thorndike. In the article Thorndike reported the results of a test based on the question: "To what extent is the strength of an interest from ten to fourteen prophetic of the strength which that interest will manifest in adult life?" Thorndike's conclusion was that interests exhibited at this age remain fairly stable throughout life. Thorndike wrote, "The importance of these facts for the whole field of practice with respect to early diagnosis, vocational guidance, the work of social secretaries, deans, advisers, and others who direct students' choices of schools, studies, and careers, is obvious."[24]

The assumption about the importance of the developing social drives and interests was related to American concepts of adolescence. One influential figure in this area was G. Stanley Hall. Hall wrote in the introduction to his classic work on adolescence in 1904, "The whole future of life depends on how the new powers [of adolescence] now given suddenly and in profusion are husbanded."[25] According to Hall's theory of recapitulation, each stage of individual development could be matched to a stage of social evolution. Childhood, the years between four and eight, corresponded to a cultural epoch when hunting and fishing were the main activities of man. From eight to twelve, according to Hall, the child recapitulated the humdrum life of savagery. During puberty the new flood of passions developed the social man. "The social instincts," Hall wrote, "undergo sudden unfoldment and the new life of love awakens."[26]

Hall's theories supported arguments that adolescent interests and abilities had to be harnessed and directed to some socially useful function in society. Adolescence was the key period for developing and directing all future social actions. The ability to fulfill the function of properly utilizing adolescent drives, Hall argued, should be the means by which social institutions are evaluated. He placed his faith in the belief that the proper training of adolescents was the panacea for most social problems. The "womb, cradle, nursery, home, family, relatives, school, church, and state," Hall wrote, "are only a series of larger cradles or placenta, as the soul . . . builds itself larger missions, the only test and virtue of which is their service in bringing the youth to ever fuller maturity."[27] One recommendation that he made was that adolescents be protected from the evil influences of modern civilization and organized into boys' clubs under the guidance of adults. These social organizations were to utilize the natural instincts of youth and "so direct intelligence and will as to secure the largest measure of social service, advance altruism, and reduce selfishness, and thus advance the higher cosmic order."[28]

Hall's view on the relationship between developing adolescent sexual drives and social abilities reflected popular attitudes. Jane Addams called the "divine fire" of youth a "sex susceptibility which suffuses the world with its deepest meaning and beauty, and furnishes the momentum towards all art. . . ."[29] She felt that the cheap commercialism of the dance halls and flashing lights of the city streets channeled the spirit of youth in the wrong direction. In a book published in 1909 she argued that it was the "fundamental susceptibility of sex which now so bewilders the street life and drives young people themselves into all sorts of difficulties. . . ."[30] Her solution was to direct the energies of youth away from the streets and into parks, playgrounds, parades, education, and national ceremonies. The divine fire of youth, Jane Addams believed, should be directed toward the problems of the world. The youthful quest for beauty and impatience with the world's wrongs would purify the social order. The spirit of youth recaptured from the shoddy commercialism of modern society could be properly tended "into a lambent flame with power to make clean our dingy streets."[31]

Probably the most popular expression of this attitude toward adolescence was Booth Tarkington's 1915 novel, *Seventeen*. Tarkington directly linked the developing sexual drives with a growing social awareness and defined adolescence as the most important stage of social growth. For seventeen, Tarkington wrote, "is the time of life when one finds it unendurable not to seem perfect in all outward matters: in worldly position, in the equipments of wealth, in family, and in the grace, elegance, and dignity of all appearances in public."[32] Through the course of the novel seventeen-year-old William Baxter is led from one comic situation to another. All of them center around the problems of adolescence and love. Tarkington portrays Baxter as being driven by his sexual instincts to acts of tenderness, poetry, social adjustment, and nobility. Near the end of the novel when William's summer sweetheart was about to leave and he was standing watching the final party and dreaming of his love, Tarkington gave full expression to the romantic view of adolescence. He wrote, "For seventeen needs only some paper lanterns, a fiddle, and a pretty girl—and Versailles is all there!"[33]

This conception of the importance of adolescence clearly affected education. It provided further justification for separating the upper years of grammar school into a school with a different type of education. It also meant that vocational guidance would concentrate on the developing social instincts of adolescence. One example of the type of educational distinctions being made because of this concept of adolescence was the 1911 report of the National Education Association's Committee on a System of Teaching Morals in the Public Schools. The committee's report was essentially a description of how the pupil in each grade should be educated for participation in social life. There was a marked difference in methods proposed between the upper and lower grades. The reason given was that adolescence was "the time of life when passion is born which must be restrained and guided aright or it consumes soul and body. It is the time when social interests are dominant and when social ideals are formed."[34] The concept that real social development was a phenomenon of adolescence led the committee to propose just for the lower grades the inculcation of good moral habits through mechanical routine. For instance, instructions for the second grade recommended training in obedience by "obeying directions given in reference to conduct and school work." For the high school grades the report suggested that the social instincts should be molded in cooperative social activities, student government, and a curriculum geared to showing the social relationships between the individual and society.[35]

In the popular educational language of the period the junior high school age of twelve to fifteen was called the "gang period." One writer on the junior high school project in 1916 stated that the advantage of the new institution was that it took account of the "nature and upheaval at the dawn of the teens which makes the pubescent ferment." In his opinion the serious defect of the eight year grammar school was that secondary education began "at too late a period in the child's life—at the age of fourteen." The age of twelve he referred to as "a period of 'fulminating psychic expansion.'" The "fulminating psychic expansion" of the gang period involved the early development of a desire to form groups and participate in cooperative activities.[36] One student of G. Stanley Hall defined the gang age as between ten and sixteen and referred to it as the "earliest manifestation in man of that strange group-forming instinct, without which beehive and ant hill and human society would be alike impossible."[37] Hall's student, J. Adams Puffer, published a book on *The Boy and His Gang* based on case histories he had collected as principal of the Lyman School for Boys in Boston in the early 1900's. Under Hall's influence Puffer argued that the gang age corresponded to a tribal period in the development of man which "began somewhere this side of the glacial period, and came to an end with, let us say, the early middle ages." Gang crime was caused by cultural evolution outdistancing biological evolution. Apparent anti-social gang activities resulted from archaic racial instincts. Puffer noted that most crime committed by gangs centered around the stealing of food. The stealing of pears, cakes, and bananas was the result of tribal predatory instincts. The solution to these problems, Puffer argued, was not to disband the gang, but to channel gang instincts into clubs and the boy scouts.[38]

The junior high school age was therefore to be developed by both vocational guidance and differentiation, and by channeling and molding social instincts. Principal Cox of the Ben Blewett Junior High School referred to his teachers as "members of gangs" and wrote that "gang loyalty makes the teacher a far more powerful leader than he could be if he depended on his authority and obedience of children."[39] The emphasis on socialization further supported the idea that guidance involved vocational goals and character adjustment. One of the first junior high schools in Philadelphia devoted the last period on Friday to personal guidance or, as it was referred to, "direct moral guidance." This school was typical of most junior high schools in that its personal guidance was linked to school activities. The guidance program was "tied up, as all guidance is, with the daily privileges and duties of the varying school lives of the pupils." At this particular junior high school there was a student government and one hundred student organizations. To accommodate these activities within the school day a seventh period was added. The student organizations provided socialization training while the seventh period on Friday was devoted to analysis of the individual effectiveness of the activities programs.[40]

Socialization in the junior high school received widespread support. C. O. Davis made a survey of junior high schools in the North Central Association territory in 1917 and 1918. Davis found that the junior high school had been "developed largely because it lends itself better than does the older type of school to the multiple needs of many classes of pupils. . . ." The response to Davis's survey was not completely favorable to the junior high. Without stating reasons why the support was not a hundred percent, Davs reported that of the 293 schools answering his questionnaire 67.91 percent believed that the junior high school was positively advantageous. With regard to socialization more principals felt the junior high could handle this problem than reacted positively to the whole junior high school concept. Of the 293 schools reporting, 69.62 percent stated that the junior high school tended "to produce better socially equipped pupils."[41]

The wedding of vocational guidance and socialization in the junior high school provided the complete educational program for the new corporate system. Differentiation would prepare the student for a particular place in society and socialization would teach the student to cooperate and work for the good of the entire organization. One example of this combination was the Ben Blewett Junior High School. The principal of the school claimed that teachers could differ with him on anything except "the two fundamental principles for which the school stands." The two principles that demanded everyone's loyalty were differentiation and socialization. These were, Principal Cox claimed, the two "fundamental purposes" which directed the original organization and development of the school. The first principle stated the need for a differentiated curriculum. The second stated that "the school cannot be a preparation for adult social life except as it reproduces within itself situations typical of social life. . . ."[42]

The junior high school socialization program placed the same emphasis on social conformity as had socialized recitation. One enthusiastic supporter wrote in the May, 1919 issue of the *Educational Review* that a new spirit would pervade the junior high school. "This spirit will be the spirit of cooperation, the spirit of service and of sacrifice for the common good." The junior high age was important because, "Those who know the nature of children are aware that the junior high school period coincides with the time when the social instincts begin to assert themselves with great force."[43] The vehicle for the new social spirit was extra-curricular cooperative group activities. The socialization programs centered around a system of school clubs. For example, a survey in 1922 of the nine years of development of New York junior high schools showed that there were 387 clubs and 68 other after school activities in operation. The clubs ranged from 83 centering around physical training to 31 devoted to history projects.[44]

The ideological support for the club system of socialization was based on the two ideas of developing adolescent interests and social instincts. The function of the clubs, like the function of the whole junior high school, was to capture and channel these new drives. Extra-curricular activities, by bringing the pupils together on an informal basis, gave them a chance to learn how to cooperate and work together. The opening sentence of the section of the survey on after school activities of the New York junior high schools read, "One of the prominent characteristics of adolescent boys and girls is the broadening of social relations in contrast to the limited social circle of the pre-adolescent age." Because clubs centered around a specific activity, they also helped to guide developing interests. This, of course, was the justification used for the vocational guidance of the junior high age. The New York survey reflected this attitude in stating, "Another prominent characteristic of adolescent boys and girls is the appearance of interests of various kinds, such as interest in literature, in science, in arts. . . ."[45]

The organizational center for club activities and guidance in most schools was the homeroom period. The development of this educational institution paralleled that of the junior high school. Like most educational innovations of the period it developed its own supporting ideology. One basic argument given for the homeroom was that the junior high school student tended to be lost and confused by departmental teaching. The homeroom was to provide a "home" where the student could seek direction and advice. The principal of the Garfield Junior High in Richmond, Indiana, wrote, "The work of teacher-advisers—or home-room teachers, as they are sometimes called—is to unify the school life of the pupil. . . ."[46] But giving the student a home led to a debate over whether the homeroom should be mixed or homogeneous. Those who supported a mixed group from various grades, vocational tracks, and social backgrounds argued as the principal of the Garfield School did: "It makes for solidarity and for breadth of interest on the part of pupils."[47] Others argued that the homeroom could only feel like a home if the pupils were homogeneous. One writer from a Cleveland high school stated that the composition of homerooms should be by neighborhoods. This attitude reflected the problem of "young people of foreign birth or parentage." The writer argued, "To be comfortable and to be yourself you want to choose your friends and mingle socially with those with whom you are congenial. This presupposes a certain common background of experiences. . . ."[48] The advisory function of the homeroom was moral and vocational. Some people thought the period was so important as a moral and social guide that they argued, as did a writer in the *Junior High School Clearing House,* "It should come at the beginning of the day. It needs to be carefully planned for its influence should and will carry throughout the day."[49] The homerooms also functioned as clearing houses for all the school's club activities. The Washington Junior High School in Rochester, New York, organized its fifty-two homerooms into one large organization which included all school clubs. The homerooms functioned as the basic unit of this school organization. The school motto was "Do in Cooperation."[50]

The junior high school was often referred to as an experiment in democracy. What this meant was that the school attempted to develop individual abilities and interests through guidance, social activities, and a differentiated curriculum. A common phrase among educational writers was "meeting the needs of the individual." This was a very restricted definition of democracy because individualism in this context meant doing an individualized task for the good of society. Within the junior high school individualization meant accepting that educational program which was believed best suited to develop individual capabilities. It was assumed to be almost an obligation to society to accept training for those abilities discovered by the guidance counselor. Democracy did not involve choice but rather doing that which you were best able to do. This definition of democracy became very inflexible and limiting when it was assumed that there was a permanency of interests during adolescence.

CHAPTER SIX

THE COMPREHENSIVE HIGH SCHOOL AND SOCIALIZATION

S pecialization in the schools threatened the goal of socialization. In providing different courses of studies the school created the same problem of social isolation caused by specialization that had faced other institutions. Educators believed that like the factory worker on the assembly line, the student in separate courses of study was losing a sense of unity and interdependence. A differentiated course of study directly threatened the whole goal of training a self-sacrificing and cooperative individual. Specialization in the schools could not be abandoned for socialization because they were both a part of the same image of a corporate society. Educating a cooperative individual to do his own little part for the whole society required both forms of education. The ideal was an educational institution that balanced the two goals. It was for this reason that the suggestions made for separate trade schools were usually rejected. The generally accepted solution to the problem was the comprehensive high school.

The basic principle of the comprehensive high school was the maintenance of a differentiated program within one institution with unity and socialization being the result of extra-curricular activities. The activities program offered the same organizational solutions that had been used in factory welfare programs. Since unity was not inherent within a separated educational program, it had to be imposed. The methods paralleled markedly the factory activities of clubs, outings, assemblies, magazines, and the other means used to create a corporate spirit. In the American high school it was clubs, athletics, assemblies, student government, and school newspapers. These, in fact, became the symbols of what a high school in America was all about.

The classic statement for the comprehensive high school was the Cardinal Principles of Secondary Education issued by a special committee of the National Education Association in 1918. The report, which was widely distributed and discussed, was written during a period when demands were being made for highly differentiated curriculums. These demands ranged from provisions for separate trade schools to differentiation based on social and economic backgrounds. For instance, Charles Hughes Johnston of the University of Illinois argued that differentiated curriculums should be planned and based "upon social rather than necessarily vague psychological considerations."[1] When the Cardinal Principles report did appear, it was criticized by educators like David Snedden for proposing a school that could give only an imitation of vocational education. Snedden believed that real vocational training required specialized schools.[2] Considering the strong pressures for differentiation the report was, as Edward Krug has shown, rather mild and compromising.[3]

The report proposed that "differentiation should be, in the broad sense of the term, vocational . . . such as agricultural, business, clerical, industrial, fine-arts, and household-arts curriculums." It supported the idea of a junior high school but limited its functions to exploration of vocations and prevocational guidance. This meant that systematic and organized differentiation of students would not take place in the junior high school but would be postponed to the senior high school. The junior high was defined as a period of exploration while the senior high was one of training. Both the junior and senior high schools were to be comprehensive, the junior high because it would aid "the pupil through a wide variety of contacts and experiences to obtain a basis for intelligent choice of his educational and vocational career," and the senior high because it would assure the choice of a curriculum best suited to the student's needs. The committee reasoned that specialized schools might introduce distracting influences such as location, athletic teams, and friends. These influences, rather than consideration of curriculum, might determine which school the student attended. The comprehensive high school, in the opinion of the committee, would eliminate these factors from consideration. Everyone would attend the same school regardless of their choice of course of study.

The comprehensive high school also allowed for what the committee called the two components of democracy, specialization and unification. The report stated, "The purpose of democracy is so to organize society that each member may develop his personality primarily through activities designed for the well-being of his fellow members and of society as a whole." The specialized and differentiated curriculum of the school was to train the individual to perform some task in society that would be for the good of society. This definition of democracy and education was very similar to the one that permeated the vocational guidance and junior high school movements. Democracy was viewed primarily as a means of social organization which allowed everyone to do what he was best able to do. Education was to fit the individual for a social position that would allow for his maximum contribution to society. In bold type the report stated, "education in a democracy, . . . should develop in each individual the knowledge, interests, ideals, habits, and powers whereby he will find his place and use that place to shape both himself and society toward ever nobler ends."

Unification was that part of the ideal of democracy that brought men together and gave them "common ideas, common ideals, and common modes of thought, feeling, and action that made for cooperation, social cohesion, and social solidarity." The report argued that in other countries social solidarity was achieved through common heredity, a centralized government, and an established religion. In America, with its diverse reli-

gious and ethnic backgrounds, "the members of different vocations often fail to recognize the interests that they have in
common with others." The one major agency in the United
States to achieve this purpose, using an argument that went
back to the founding fathers, was the school. In terms of the
current concepts of childhood the unifying force had to be the
secondary school and not the elementary school, for only during
adolescence did the social instincts begin forming. The report
stated, "In this process the secondary school must play an
important part because the elementary school with its imma-
ture pupils cannot alone develop the common knowledge, common ideals, and common interests essential to American democracy."

To compensate for the separation caused by the different
courses of study the committee proposed three means of
creating a sense of unity. The first, which was directed toward
the immigrant, emphasized the need for teaching the "mother
tongue" and social studies. The other two were organizational
techniques. One was "social mingling of pupils through the
organization and administration of the school." The last was
directly related to this proposal. The committee called for the
"participation of pupils in common activities . . . , such as
athletic games, social activities, and the government of the
school."[4]

The two organizational techniques of creating social solidarity became popularly known in the 1920's as extra-curricular
activities. The various phases of school life that came under
this term were in existence long before the issuance of the
Cardinal Principles Report. But during the 1920's extra-
curricular activities developed into an educational cult. Courses
in organizing extra-curricular activities were offered in teacher
training institutions. Textbooks and books of readings on the
topic were published. In 1926 the *Twenty-Fifth Yearbook of
the National Society for the Study of Education* was devoted to
the topic "of extra-curricular education." Like any educational
movement certain figures emerged as leaders. One in particular
was Elbert K. Fretwell of Teachers College. Fretwell organized
summer courses at Teachers College for school administrators so

that they could perfect their extra-curricular programs. Between 1923 and 1926 Fretwell flooded the *Teachers College Record* with long bibliographies of material on assemblies, clubs, student government, and homerooms.[5] A serious debate also occurred during this period over how extra-curricular, extra-curricular activities should be. Educators, like Thomas Briggs of Teachers College, argued that extra-curricular activities should be included in the regular curricular schedule because this would "raise these activities to the place of dignity and respect that they deserve as an educational feature of the school in the eyes of pupils, teachers, and community."[6]

One of the sources of inspiration for the extra-curricular activity movement was Dewey's idea that the school should be a community with a real social life. This idea had developed through the years into the idea that the school had to provide a social activities program. One aspect of this idea was that the child would learn by doing. In other words the social activities program provided concrete situations for the development of social skills and a working set of ethics. An assumption underlying this argument was that the school was responsible for the education of the whole child. This position had been assumed by American schools at the turn of the century with the extension of school activities. In an often quoted speech William Bishop Owen, dean of the University of Chicago High School, in 1906 expressed this sentiment before a group of high school and academy administrators. He told them, "It is the whole pupil who goes to school. This can be made true only on condition that the school cares for all the interests which govern the child's life while he is under the influence of the school." One interesting and extremely perceptive parallel made by Owen was between the school and the factory. Owen stated, "Gradually it is coming to be recognized that it is the whole man who goes into the factory in the morning and out in the evening; that merely to serve the selfish purpose of the employer it is necessary to provide for the whole man, physical, intellectual, moral, aesthetic, and social."[7]

The basic goal of learning by doing and educating the whole man was to produce a unified, cooperative populace with common ideals and goals. The referent, as in the Cardinal Principles, was always a concept of democracy which included personal sacrifice to the state and a social organization which allowed for the most efficient use of individual talents. In the eyes of educators this concept of democracy justified including in the schools activities ranging from student government to assemblies. Student government, for instance, was to be the new training ground for democracy, while "through school assemblies and organizations," in the words of the Cardinal Principles report, "they acquire common ideas."[8]

Extra-curricular activities were also to turn the school into an ideal democratic community. One very popular statement of the period was that the school must become a democracy. The Cardinal Principles report went one step further and stated flatly that "the comprehensive school is the prototype of a democracy in which various groups must have a degree of self-consciousness as groups and yet be federated into a larger whole through the recognition of common interests and ideals."[9] Statements of this nature are very revealing because they suggest that one thing that can be determined from an investigation of the organization of the schools is the image educators had of a democracy.

The central feature of all social activities programs was student government. The important place student government assumed in the public schools resulted from activities of urban reform groups in New York City in the 1890's. At the time student government was hailed as the great salvation for the democratic process. The early leader of the movement was Wilson Gill, a Columbus, Ohio, industrialist who sometime between 1874 and 1889 decided to devote his life to reforming municipal politics. The decision was occasioned by the defeat of a proposal to introduce industrial training into the schools. Gill claimed that the "project was defeated at the polls by the vote of ignorant men, under the direction of ward heelers."[10] His early educational attempts to correct this evil were devoted to forming the Sons of the American Revolution in 1889. Gill claimed the distinction of writing the constitutions for both the Sons and Daughters of the American Revolution.[11] These two

groups were formed originally as Americanization organizations. The pages of the proceedings of these two organizations
reflected an attempt to solve the problem of the "ward heeler"
through patriotic education. One of the stated objectives of the
Sons of the American Revolution was the encouragement of
"such education as will best prepare our children for the dis-
charge of the important duties of American citizenship. . . ."[12]
The meaning of this objective was made clear at the Second
Annual Congress of the S.A.R. in 1891 when the president of
the New York chapter stated to the gathered delegates, "We
want the immigrant of yesterday to say with the descendant of
the soldier of the Revolution, 'My pride and inspiration . . . is
George Washington.' "[13] Along with his work in these patriotic
groups Gill campaigned for other educational programs. For
instance, in 1888 he claimed that he secured for educational
purposes an "act of Congress requiring that the name of the
person represented by a portrait on paper money and other
government documents shall be printed with the portrait."
Later this included postage stamps.[14]

Gill eventually became a crusader for student government
when he abandoned the Sons and Daughters of the Revolution
because they did not spend enough time working with the
public schools. He formed in New York City in 1891 the
American Patriotic League. The roster of the members of the
American Patriotic League included such illustrious names as
Rutherford B. Hayes, William McKinley, Theodore Roosevelt,
Josiah Strong, Leonard Wood, and John R. Commons. As president of the organization Wilson Gill developed under his
editorship an extensive Americanization program in the form
of *Our Country* magazine. During its early years of publication
the magazine was designed to provide the reader with a three-
year course in American citizenship. Later this goal was abandoned and the last issue was devoted exclusively to student
government. The educational program of *Our Country* reflected
the close relationship that would exist between student government and proposals to reform the administration of urban
government. The original plan called for a chapter of a serial-
ized book to appear in each monthly magazine. The list of

topics that were covered ranged from citizenship and history to economics and sociology. The articles that comprised this course of study were not purely flag-waving statements. Frederic W. Speirs, professor of political economy at the Drexel Institute, wrote a series of articles that were highly critical of the American system of laissez-faire capitalism. He criticized the system for creating unemployment, turning the worker into an automaton, and exploiting child labor. Articles by John R. Commons called for reform of municipal government and the institution of proportional representation. Other reform statements included: Edward Everett Hale on the need for an international supreme court; Theodore Roosevelt on civil service reform; and one whole issue devoted to George E. Waring and his war against dirty streets in New York and Cuba.

After several years as editor, Wilson Gill decided that no great quantity of printed arguments would ever be completely effective. This he decided was why the public schools were not turning out good citizens. There was a great deal of talk about democracy within school walls but very little practice. Writing in the last issue of *Our Country* in 1899 Gill asked, "What is the matter with Americans whose brains have been cultivated?" His reply to his own question was, "As long as one remains in school, he is subject to school government, which is monarchical in form and effect. . . ."[15] He decided the real answer to the problem of the "ward heeler" and corrupt urban politics was training youth in democracy, later called a democratic apprenticeship program. Gill began his campaign for student self-government in 1897 when, after several visits to the classroom of a schoolteacher member of the American Patriotic League, he organized a "school city." The classroom was located in a school which was described as having students who were so unruly that Police Commissioner Theodore Roosevelt had to detail policemen to patrol it. The teacher of the classroom later stated in a book published in 1907 that while he had developed a system of self-government in his classroom it did not take on a meaningful form until Wilson Gill became interested.[16]

Gill's original plan called for the organization of the school along the lines of a model city government. This was called a "school city." Later plans were based on federal and state governments. Under the school city plan the pupils were granted a charter which gave them the power to elect a mayor, a president of the council, a city council, and clerk of the court. The mayor was to appoint commissioners of health, public works, and police. Gill wanted this plan to serve as a training ground for a democracy organized along reformist lines. In the final issue of *Our Country* he suggested that the initiative, the referendum, proportional representation, and primary reform be included in all school city organizations. He also suggested that those establishing a school city consult John R. Commons' *Proportional Representation*.[17] The New York reform mayor, William Strong, took an interest in the school city project and appointed Alfred Beebe, the assistant director of Diagnosis Bacteriological Laboratory of the New York City Board of Health, to develop a school city health department. The plan called for providing information on health practices and student supervision and control of the sanitary conditions of the schools. Each school city was to appoint food sanitary inspectors who would check on the health and cleanliness of fellow students, and the condition and quality of all food entering the schools.[18]

When *Our Country* ceased publication in 1899, Gill began to spend most of his time on school city projects. At the turn of the century he was assigned by the War Department to organize the schools of Cuba into School Republics. After his Cuban adventure he was hired by the Department of Interior as a commissioner-at-large to organize student governments in Indian schools.[19] The idea of student government as a cure for the ills of democracy spread through other sources. A member of the American Patriotic League and editor of the *Review of Reviews*, Albert Shaw tried in 1899, the same year as the closing of *Our Country*, to find the extent of student self-government in the public schools. Shaw reported in an article titled, "The School City—A Method of Pupil Self-Government," that a form of the school city was being used in schools in Philadelphia, Chicago, Milwaukee, and Omaha. Articles on student government also began appearing in educational journals.[20] In 1898 and 1900 C. W. French, principal of the Hyde Park High School, contributed articles to the *School Review* praising the citizenship and moral training values of student government.[21]

It was 1904 that marked the real beginning of an organized national campaign for student government. In that year Richard Welling, another New York reformer, organized the National Self-Government Committee. This organization eventually listed such illustrious members as Nicholas Murray Butler, John Dewey, Alfred Smith, William McAndrew, Harry Emerson Fosdick, and Stephen S. Wise. The organization campaigned vigorously into the 1940's for student government not only in the public schools but also in colleges and universities. Welling's reasons for founding the committee were very similar to the ones that had led Gill to devote his life to organizing student governments. Up to 1903 Welling had spent many frustrating years working for urban reform in New York City. After graduating in 1880 from Harvard where he had been a classmate of Theodore Roosevelt and had taught Sunday School with him, Welling studied for a law degree and returned to New York. In 1882 Welling along with Theodore Roosevelt and others formed the City Reform Club to wage war against Tammany Hall. Welling devoted a great deal of his time both to the Reform Club and to the political campaigns of reform mayors like William Strong and Seth Low. In 1894 he participated in the founding of the National Municipal League. Through much of his work he shared common political interests and contacts with Wilson Gill and the American Patriotic League.[22]

Welling claimed that in 1903 he finally realized that education was the key to civic reform. He lamented that merely "telling the voters that their taxes were too high did not lead to action at the polls."[23] The best method, he decided, was to give the citizen an opportunity to practice the intelligent use of his political rights. Having reached this conclusion he contacted Charles Eliot, the president of the National Education Association, and asked permission to address the annual convention of the association. Before the convention he made a ringing appeal for instituting student government to help cure corrupt government. He told the gathered educators, "The New generation must be imbued with a new spirit of civic patriotism . . . you must teach the machinery of the government by means of some form of applied civics. . . ." The applied civics he suggested was the "noble effort making in the School City . . . designed to bring about the very contact [between student and government] by converting the school itself into a municipality. . . ."[24]

Student governments were instituted by American schools at a phenomenal rate. By the middle of the century there were very few junior or senior high schools that did not have some form of democratic organization. Through the course of development there was never any serious suggestion that the students be given real power. The purpose was to provide applied civics, not to run the school. A typical attitude was that taken by William McAndrew, one time superintendent of the New York public schools. Writing in 1897 on a proposed student government plan he stated, "I believe the plan of delegating any of the executive powers of that officer (principal) to those so irresponsible as students must be would be unwise."[25] There was general agreement, at least among educators during this period, that, as one writer stated, "any plan that gives pupils full control of the government of a school, a school city, or a school democracy, without the advice and aid of teachers will necessarily lead to an ignominious failure."[26]

Student government, therefore, never provided training in the exercise of power but only in the mechanical details. During student elections the pupil learned the details and methods of political conventions, campaigning, balloting, and vote counting. In student councils and courts he learned procedures and parliamentary rules. But through the course of all these activities the student never had any real contact with power. All of the government activities took place in a vacuum without real issues. The student learned the procedural methods of democracy, not that democracy involved a constant struggle. Some educators actually worried that if the students found out they had no real power, the whole student government method would fail. One writer in 1916 described pupil self-government as "the government of pupils by pupils under the invisible direction of teachers. . . ." He then went on to wonder if student government didn't often fail "because the teachers are not skillful enough to keep their direction of affairs invisible."[27]

Student government was also attractive because it provided what was often called a democratic form of discipline. This meant control through assent to school rules or judgments made by peers. But since the pupil never had any real power over school policies, this made his assent a very subtle form of control. One article on student government stated in 1918 that the basic reason for the plan was discipline. The article described discipline as "a matter of internal adjustment, spontaneous internal control and [it] does not properly get its significance when it is obtained by means of force or by any suppressive measures."[28] This argument was fairly typical. Meaningful discipline was impossible if it had to be conveyed by force. But if it were accepted by agreement to school rules, then it became internalized and consequently, was more effective.

If student government was to be the heart of the prototypic democratic community, meaning the American high school, it suggests that democracy was primarily thought of as a way to maintain effective social order. New York urban reformers, it will be recalled from an earlier chapter, were interested in making adjustments in the political system so that it would limit the participation of lower social and economic groups. Their major concern was that these groups learn how to operate the machinery of government properly. The same thing was true of student government. The pupils were given the chance to agree with the executive power of the school. Democracy in this sense was a positive way of maintaining allegiance to the laws. This concept was similar to the one suggested by vocational guidance and the junior high school. The image of democracy in those cases was of a social system that allowed everyone the opportunity to exercise his best talents for the good of society. Democracy, as it was reflected in student government, was an effective way of maintaining social order. Both images blended to suggest that the ideal democracy was a smooth running machine with social order and cohesion maintained through universal, yet voluntary allegiance to common social goals.

The other organizations that made up the extra-curricular activities program had less colorful histories and were not as directly related to political reform. They were still justified in terms of their contribution to unifying the school and preparing students for a cooperative democracy. In most plans the student government or student association was to work in cooperation with the faculty in the administration of any programs. The other activities usually included a student newspaper, clubs, athletics, and assemblies. One principal stated in 1917 that an organized program of this nature would "assist in making the spirit of democracy, 'all for each and each for all,' to pervade the entire school."[29]

The school newspaper served a variety of functions. On the one hand it was a means of teaching English. As a teaching method it was supported by all the current educational rhetoric of learning by doing. On the other hand it taught teamwork and created a spirit of unity in the school. Publication of a paper, like any school club activity, was viewed as an important means of teaching people how to work effectively in groups. The school newspaper contributed to a sense of unity by providing each student with news about school events. Some supporters of school newspapers considered this to be its most important function. One of them wrote: "The Press Association . . . meets an important demand. It is a unifying organization, and is therefore a wholesome factor if properly directed. Its purpose is to edit a school paper through which a school spirit may be awakened and nourished."[30] The school newspaper through a combination of gossip and pep talk was to fill a role very much like that of factory publications. The student through reading the paper was to gain a sense of the unity of school life and a feeling of loyalty to the educational programs. To a certain extent the paper was to be a public relations method of building a good image in the student's eyes. As one writer stated, "The school paper . . . will create school patriotism and an increased interest in all the activities of the school, educational, athletic, and social."[31]

Clubs in school programs eventually ranged over a variety of areas including academic, athletic, and vocational. Most high schools and academies in the nineteenth century had some social organizations, usually literary and debating societies. The difference at the early part of the twentieth century was not only the broad range of clubs that developed but also the fact that they were justified in terms of teaching people how to cooperate. As was noted in an earlier chapter, this argument was usually made in terms of the developing interests and social instincts of adolescents. After the 1918 Cardinal Principles report, the argument that clubs served as preparation for worthy use of leisure frequently appeared. This was similar to the factory owner's concern about his workers' activities after working hours. One of the suggested purposes of education in the Cardinal Principles report had been the development of meaningful leisure-time activities. It was stated in one article on club activities in 1924, "A school's service to the future makers of America does not end with preparing them for working hours which occupy only a third of the day. It must also provide specifically for the worthy use of leisure."[32] The school's responsibility not only was to turn out efficient workers and citizens but also people who played efficiently.

It was argued that athletics could contribute to training for a democratic community in two ways. One way was as part of a general health program that would assure individual physical efficiency. The Cardinal Principles, in language that suggested that the individual was being viewed as a piece of national resource, stressed health as an important educational objective. A good physical-training program in the school would produce a strong and well-functioning laborer. Athletics also taught the student how to cooperate and work with a team. This was one reason for the rapid growth of football in the public schools. As a team game it represented all the coordination and cooperation needed in a corporate organization. A principal of a Seattle (Washington) high school told the National Education Association in 1915, "In the boy's mind, the football team is not only an aggregation of individuals organized to play, but a social instrument with common needs, working along common lines, and embodying a common purpose. . . ."[33] The socializing function was an important factor in the introduction of athletic programs in junior high schools. A great deal of the time in these programs was directed to some form of competitive group game. The reason for this, as given by two members of the Skokie, Illinois school system, was "to stimulate greater interest on the part of the children and at the same time to be able to stress the elements of cooperation or team work essential for successful competitive activity."[34]

The spirit generated by athletic games between schools was considered another means of uniting the student body. It also served an important public relations function and united the entire community around the school. Every boy's dad would be willing to attend the local football game. The problem as seen by one professor of physical education in 1914 was maintaining a balance between the individual efficiency aspect of athletics and the entertainment of spectators. He felt very confident at this time that the balance could be achieved. Fifteen years ago, he wrote, high school athletes were "accustomed to playing a game unrestrained and without cooperation. All sorts of tricks were used to win a contest, such as importing players, choosing biased officials, and resorting to unfair tactics in general. . . . Today our athletes from the high schools represent the best sportsmanship possible."[35] The success of football in uniting the community and generating spirit eventually unbalanced these two purposes. In 1923 a high school teacher complained, "Rivalry between certain schools has become so intense that players meet in a spirit of hatred and revenge, and special policing is necessary to guard against outbreaks of hostility between rival rooters." The writer reported that athletics had become so important that in Ohio many athletes "attend school periodically and only for special sports. They are never ineligible, and some of them have been in high-school athletics for a long term of years, shifting from school to school in order to conform to the letter of the rules."[36]

The extra-curricular activity that was believed would fully

unify the school was the assembly. Historically the assembly probably descended from the school chapel. By the 1920's it was hailed as the great unifier of the comprehensive junior and senior high schools. One of the early assembly programs, and one often discussed by educators, was the morning exercise of the Francis W. Parker School in Chicago. During the 1880's Francis Parker would begin each day at the Cook County Normal School by reading to the entire faculty and staff a short passage from the Bible or a book of poetry. Following the reading a group of students would present an exercise that was usually the outcome of classwork. The practice was continued after the Francis Parker School was founded in 1901.[37] The school believed that the morning exercise provided the best basis for bringing the school together as a corporate body. The 1913 yearbook of the school referred to the exercise as "the family altar of the school to which each brings his offerings—the fruits of his observations and studies. . . ."[38] Before the family altar the child had the opportunity to become aware of the entire school. Through the years the important function of the exercise was to counteract the feelings of separation caused by the students being divided into different grades. The 1913 yearbook of the school stated, "The morning exercise is one means of impressing upon the children the unity of the whole school and of counteracting some of the undesirable effects of the separation into grades."[39]

This was precisely why the Cardinal Principles report recommended the assembly as a school unifier. The common argument given was that as the school was divided into separate grades, courses of studies, and ability groups, some means had to be found to create a corporate feeling. An associate superintendent of schools in Pittsburgh, Pennsylvania, wrote in 1925, "Students are divided into classes according to their academic advancement, further divided by their curricula. . . . Blocking the pathway to unity is an almost infinite variety of individual differences. The assembly is the one agency at hand capable of checking these tendencies."[40] Assemblies were one of the great events in the American junior and senior high schools. Books, programs, and articles flooded the educational market with suggestions for auditorium exercises. Band concerts, vocational talks, drama productions, class projects, and patriotic celebrations all became part of the public school paraphernalia. The theme of the assembly unifying a diverse educational program continued through the 1920's. At the very opening of the book, *Assemblies for Junior and Senior High Schools,* published in 1929, was stated, "Junior and senior high schools daily accept the challenge to prepare students for life in a democracy. . . . Specialized organization and complex activities necessitate unification through athletics, the school newspaper, and the assembly. Because of its frequency and provision for universal participation, the assembly may be considered the foremost integrating factor."[41]

The desire to create a cooperative and unified spirit reflected the nature of the democratic aspirations of educators. The *Fifth Yearbook of the Department of Secondary-School Principals* in 1921 stated with regard to extra-curricular activities, "What we wish the state to be the school must be. The character of our citizens is determined by the character of our pupils and the development of character in this broadest sense must be the goal of education."[42] The socialized classroom and school activities had as their goal a cooperative man who was willing to dedicate himself to the benefit of the state. At times this goal bordered on the totalitarian idea that the state was in fact something greater than the individuals who composed it. The organizational images that permeated the discussions often suggested that the institutions of society had a life of their own. Referring to an attitude of self-sacrifice learned through school activities, one educator commented, "Such an attitude leads the student body to recognize that the school is an institution greater than the pupils attending it at any time, greater than the faculty that happens to control its destiny at a given period, greater than the principal presiding at the moment."[43]

The parallels that can be drawn between the socialization programs of the factory and school are not accidental. Both believed they faced the problem of internal fragmentation and both believed that the new institutions of society required a cooperative individual. Essentially the same image of the needs and organization of society was reflected in their socialization programs. They also shared the same goal of a society of well organized industrial combinations. They differed only in terms of their organizational position in the total social process. The schools produced the people for the system and the system produced the products.

Educators were often so concerned about the need for a particular type of well-rounded personality that they put social training above the academic. During the 1920's this became quite prevalent. Points for service to the school became at times more important than academic grades. Special assemblies were held to give service awards that many times were based on nothing but participation in school activities. Typical of this attitude during the 1920's was the proposal made before the National Education Association in 1921 for keeping a written social record for every student. The proponent of this idea asserted "that such a record kept for four years would furnish more reliable information about the efficiency of Mary's school life, her chances of success in college, in business, or as a housewife, than would the 93.6 percent that places her on the honor roll of the commencement program."[44]

CHAPTER SEVEN

THE RADICAL REACTION TO THE PUBLIC SCHOOLS

Our educational system is not a public service," Upton Sinclair wrote in the 1920's, "but an instrument of special privilege; its purpose is not to further the welfare of mankind, but merely to keep America capitalist."[1] Sinclair, an avowed socialist and famed muckraker, reflected the growing disillusionment some Americans felt toward a public school system which was being shaped to meet the needs of the growing corporate industrial state. The discontent with the schools ranged from radical anarchists to some union groups. The result was an attempt to establish alternative systems of education. Before and after World War I discontent with industrial domination of the schools bred a series of experimental schools designed as models to counteract the reactionary nature of the public schools. The search for alternative forms of education to the public school was to become one of the important strands of educational development in the twentieth century.

One of the major complaints of radical school reformers during the early part of the century was that boards of education were dominated by businessmen and a business-oriented ideology. This situation was linked to the municipal reforms which through consolidation and centralization of urban school control had eliminated representation from many sectors of the population. The triumph of business control of the schools occurred at a time when the country was undergoing a wave of intense nationalism and antiradicalism. World War I provided the opportunity for superpatriots to demand total allegiance to the American cause and the destruction of radical elements. The famous Palmer raids against radicals by Attorney General Palmer represented the near hysterical reaction that gripped the country. The reaction contained not only anti-radical feelings but also anti-union feelings. These attitudes were filtered into the schools through business-oriented boards of education and resulted, for example, in the attempt by some labor groups to establish alternative schools. As George Counts stated in his study of the social composition of school boards in the 1920's, "Clearly, the fundamental motive underlying the labor-education movement is a growing distrust of the public school . . . they do not trust the instruction which society provides for them through schools controlled by boards of education composed, for the most part, of persons representing the employers' point of view."[2]

Radicals of the period argued that a conservative ideology was forced upon the curriculum and teachers were forced to adhere to a carefully prescribed political and social ideology. It was charged that the schools not only imposed a particular reactionary view of the world but also excluded all radical teachers and the rational discussion of socialist and communist alternatives. This created during the 1920's what Upton Sinclair called a "vast graveyard of radical teachers." The end result of schooling, radical critics declared, was a population educated to accept the established social order and trained for jobs in industry at the public expense.

A related and important element of the radical critique was the argument that education itself had become big business and was run for the benefit of those in charge and not for student clients. It was charged that textbook companies manipulated the appointment of local school officials and controlled, or at least heavily influenced, the actions of organizations like the National Education Association. It was also claimed that on local levels many decisions dealing with contracts were made for the benefit of particular supply companies and real estate interests. The textbook companies and real estate interests were all viewed as being part of a set of interlocking interests.

There were several well-documented studies of social class control of public education which gave support to the accusations of radicals and union leaders. The two most important ones were Scott Nearing's studies in 1916 and 1917 of the members of boards of education and college trustees and George Counts' study of *The Social Composition of Boards of Education*. These studies supported the view that American education was dominated by conservative businessmen and the bulk of the population was not represented on boards of education or among college trustees.

Scott Nearing did his study of American education after the University of Pennsylvania refused to renew his contract as assistant professor of economics for the academic year 1915–16 for what Nearing charged was the trustees' disapproval of his campaign against child labor in Pennsylvania and his active involvement in campaigns against monopolies and corrupt public utilities. The editor of a newspaper controlled by the major opponent to child labor laws denounced a lecture given by Nearing in a church "against the greedy exploitation of helpless children as sacrilege, and called on the University trustees to rid themselves of such a dangerous professor." After his dismissal, the newspapers stated that telegrams were sent to the Governor of Pennsylvania urging him not to approve the appropriation bill for the University of Pennsylvania "until the University trustees have satisfied him [the Governor] that their dismissal of Doctor Nearing is not part payment for senate votes of child labor interests in favor of the University appropriation."[3] The background and circumstances surrounding Nearing's case were typical of many battles for academic freedom resulting from academic involvement in public issues and ideological conflict with those in control of the universities.

After the University of Pennsylvania affair, Scott Nearing began his study of American education to determine exactly what forces were in control. In December 1916, he wrote to the superintendents of 131 school systems, in cities having a population in excess of 40,000 according to the 1910 census report, requesting information about the members of the boards of education.[4] He received a reply from 104 cities representing, according to his calculations, 26 percent of the population of the United States. One of the first things Nearing noted after adding up the replies was domination of school boards by males. This was an important issue for Nearing because of his involvement in the women's rights movement. He found in his sample that in large cities with populations over 500,000 twelve percent of board members were women. In cities of between 100,000 and 500,000 eight percent were women, and in cities with less than 100,000 five percent were women.

The most important part of the study dealt with occupations of board members. Nearing selected three occupational classifications for the purpose of his study. The first was business, which included merchants, manufacturers, bankers, real estate and insurance men, and officials of corporations. The second category was professional—doctors, lawyers, ministers, teachers, scientists, authors, editors, social workers, and artists. The third classification, called "miscellaneous," included the bulk of the population and covered the rest of the occupations. It was in this category that one found business clerks, mechanics, homemakers, and the blue-collar worker. Nearing found that three fourths of all board members from the reporting cities were business or professional men and that businessmen comprised more than half the total number of board members. He also found there was a concentration of occupations within the business and professional categories. There were 433 businessmen who were school board members out of a total of 967 for the 104 reporting cities. Of those classified as businessmen, 144 were merchants, 78 were manufacturers, and 104 were bankers, brokers, and real estate and insurance men. Of the 333 classified as professional, more than one third were doctors and dentists and two fifths were lawyers. Out of 967 school board positions in the study only 201 were filled by those in the "miscellaneous" group. This included 48 clerks and salesmen, 39 mechanics and wage earners, and 25 foremen. Nearing argued that in an industrial city the wage earners and clerks represent five sixths of the total number of gainfully employed persons. He concluded, "Thus more than nine tenths of the board members in the cities under consideration fall outside of the class which makes up five sixths of the population—or . . . nine tenths of the school board members of the large American cities are selected from one sixth of the gainfully occupied population. . . ."

For his study of university trustees, Nearing selected the 189 institutions in the *Educational Directory* of the Bureau of Education having an enrollment of more than 500 students.[5] Of this total, Nearing was able to obtain lists of the occupations of board members for 143 institutions. He found that of a total of 2,470 trustees only 75 were women. The total number of businessmen was 930, or more than one third. Of this total, 833 were merchants, manufacturers, corporate officials, and bankers. The professional group totaled 1,269 board members with nine tenths of them being doctors, lawyers, educators, and ministers. In the "miscellaneous" group of 271 there were 94 retired businessmen and 123 farmers. This meant that out of a total number of college board trustees of 2,470 there were only 54 in the miscellaneous group who were not farmers or retired businessmen. Of these 54 there were 3 salesmen, 46 homekeepers, 3 mechanics, and 2 librarians. Nearing argued that his study showed the business and professional world dominated the college and university world completely. He concluded his study with the remark, "A new term must be coined to suggest the idea of an educational system owned and largely supported by the people but dominated by the business world. Perhaps 'plutocratized education' will prove as acceptable as any other phrase."

Almost ten years later George Counts duplicated Nearing's study of public schools in his *The Social Composition of Boards of Education.* Counts' study involved a larger sample of 1,654 school boards with more than half of these being rural district boards of education. This provided the opportunity for comparing the composition of city and rural school control. Counts, like Nearing, found that women tended to be excluded from control of the school—only 10.2 percent of 6,653 board members in his sample were women. Of these most were in urban schools. His study also included state college and university boards of control which, like their public school counterparts, showed a high rate of discrimination against women. In terms of leadership, Counts found that in city schools the ratio of presidents to members of the board for men was one to six, while for women it was one to twenty-nine. It was also found that proprietors, professionals, and business executives dominated the boards of education in cities. In rural areas farmers represented 95 percent of the board members.

Counts attempted to give some sociological explanations for this apparent plutocratic control of education. He noted that the representation of the laboring class varied according to the size of the city. Its representation in smaller cities was twice that of larger cities. Counts argued, "As the unit under the control of the board increases in size, importance, and complexity, the elements in the population from which members may be drawn become more and more restricted and a different type of citizen is attracted to service of the board."[6] The other element contributing to this variation was the size of the school board. As the number of members decreased, the possibility of representation from all members of the population also decreased.

Counts also noted that a tradition had developed in educational administration in the twentieth century which argued for the necessity of professional and business elements controlling school boards. He claimed that one of these experts in school administration, William E. Chancellor, in 1904 "issued a pronouncement on the personal qualifications of board members so unequivocal and categorical, and withal so convincing, that it has scarcely been challenged by subsequent writers." Chancellor's unequivocal pronouncement was that the best board members were manufacturers "accustomed to dealing with bodies of men and with important business interests," "merchants, contractors, bankers, physicians," and "college graduates in any walk of life who are successful in their own affairs." Those listed as the worst board members by Chancellor were inexperienced young men, old men, unsuccessful men, politicians, newspaper men, uneducated men, "men in subordinate business positions," and women. Twelve years later, Counts noted, Ellwood P. Cubberley restated these qualifications in his book *Public School Administration*. Counts referred to Cubberley's book as "the most widely read and influential book on school administration of our generation. . . ."[7]

The studies of business control of education by Scott Nearing and George Counts received further support from Upton Sinclair. Sinclair spent two years in the early 1920's visiting twenty-five American cities and questioning, he claimed, not less than a thousand people about American education. With his notebooks full of interviews with teachers, principals, superintendents, board members, college professors, presidents, deans, regents, and trustees, and with a mass of other information plus personal anecdotes, he published in 1923 a study of American higher education called *The Goose-Step* and in 1924 a book on the public schools titled *The Goslings*. Both books had the muckraking flavor and popular style that had made him famous in his study of the meat-packing industry in *The Jungle* and the American newspaper industry in *The Brass Check*.

In both books Sinclair stressed the business domination of American education and the resulting ideological content of the schools and the use of education for business profiteering. While these themes are not necessarily connected, Sinclair considered them as closely related parts of the corruption of American capitalism. From Sinclair's perspective, the ideological line to which the schools were required to hew was precisely the one big business used to hide its economic plundering. Thus it seemed logical to Sinclair, for example, to expect, on the one hand, a large real estate firm to pressure the local schools to fire a radical teacher and demand the teaching of a conservative economic philosophy and, on the other hand, to expect that same real estate firm to manipulate the purchase of school property for its own economic advantage.

In *The Goose-Step*, Sinclair documented his claim of business repression and propaganda in higher education with endless stories about struggles for academic freedom waged against plutocratic boards of trustees. To emphasize business control of higher education he would name each school he visited after its controlling interests. In this manner the struggle for academic freedom was waged against schools with colorful new names, such as the "University of the House of Morgan" for Columbia University, the "University of Standard Oil" for the University of Chicago, the "University of Judge Gary" for Northwestern University, the "University of Automobiles" for the University of Michigan, and the "University of the Ore Trust" for the University of Minnesota. To further emphasize the interlocking nature of the control he would list during each part of his trip the connections between owners of railroads and American universities. For example, when he traveled between Harvard (University of Lee-Higginson) and the University of Pennsylvania (University of the United Gas Improvement Company) he first rode on the New York, New Haven & Hartford Railroad which "is a Morgan road with a recent Harvard overseer for chairman, a Brown trustee for vice-president, a recent Yale president for director, and a member of the Yale advisory board, a Washburn trustee, a Wellesley trustee, a Pratt Institute trustee, two Harvard visitors for directors."[8] The next part of this trip was on the Pennsylvania Railroad which he claimed had interlocking connections with Bryn Mawr, Wilson College, Carnegie Tech, and the University of Pennsylvania. And always as a final touch to his picture that the battle was against business interests in the universities, he would list the occupations of the members of the regents or boards of trustees. One example was the school Sinclair considered the most liberal in the United States, the University of Wisconsin. The president of its board of regents was A. J. Horlick, the malted milk king, and the other members included three attorneys, a physician, an anti-LaFollette candidate for governor, a wholesale grocer, a manufacturer of bathroom fixtures, and a manufacturer's wife. Sinclair wrote that "Mr. Horlick has proven his right to be numbered among the hundred percent patriots, the firm of which he is head having been indicted by the United States government and fined fifty thousand dollars for the hoarding of flour. (Query: Is malted milk made out of flour?)"[9]

At every school he visited he found evidence of suppression of academic freedom in the interest of conservative ideology. The cases ranged from the dramatic, such as the Scott Nearing Case, to examples of his own inability to gain the right to speak on college campuses. Typical of the many cases cited by Sinclair was that of Arthur Fisher, a young professor at the University of Montana (University of Anaconda) law school. Sinclair claimed Fisher had become involved with the Farmer-Labor movement and a liberal newspaper in Montana. Another newspaper, *Missoulian,* which was controlled by Anaconda, accused Fisher of being a Bolshevik and in the spring of 1921 discovered that during World War I he had given a speech in Chicago demanding that the Allies state their war aims. Sinclair wrote, "That, of course, was 'pro-German,' and the American Legion—swallowed by the Anaconda—took up the issue, and demanded Fisher's scalp." A faculty committee met during the summer of 1921 and vindicated Fisher. The chancellor, Sinclair claimed, distorted the report when it was given to the state board of education, "and he and his board and the attorney general of the state of Anaconda worked out a most ingenious solution—they gave the radical young professor a compulsory leave of absence at full pay; they forbade him to teach law at the university. . . ."[10]

Fisher's case was typical of the ideological repression Sinclair found in his travels. A not-so-typical, but dramatic and important, example of business exploitation of higher education was Sinclair's story of Ginn and Company's control of Clark University. He referred to Clark University as an academic tragedy because of its rapid demise as a center of intellectual activity following the retirement of its distinguished President G. Stanley Hall. Following Hall's retirement, Sinclair claimed, a member of the board of trustees who was also business manager of Ginn and Company arranged for the new president of Clark to be one of the authors of its best selling geography series. The new President Wallace Walter Atwood, co-author of the Frye-Atwood elementary school geographies, immediately announced that Clark University was to become a great American center for geographical studies. What actually happened, according to Sinclair, was that Clark became a publicity center for the Frye-Atwood geography series. Not only could one of its authors sign his name as President of a university, but also he could conduct summer schools and attract school people from all over the country. Sinclair wrote, "Elaborate advertising campaigns are undertaken . . . and the schoolmarms flock from all over the United States—likewise the principals and the high-up superintendents—and they meet the distinguished authors of school books, and listen to their patriotic eloquence, and go home singing the wonders of the various 'lines'" In refusing to allow Scott Nearing to speak on campus, President Atwood showed that blend of reactionary ideology and capitalistic exploitation that Sinclair felt always went together.[11]

When Sinclair wrote about the public schools in *The Goslings,* he again came to the conclusion that business domination meant ideological control and economic exploitation. The social class domination that Nearing had already found and Counts would find later resulted in giving a reactionary and antilabor tone to the public schools. One concrete example given by Sinclair was that of the Los Angeles Public Schools, which he claimed were controlled by the local Chamber of Commerce, Better America Federation, and the Merchants' and Manufacturers' Association. The Los Angeles schools announced a Chamber of Commerce Week during which the children of the first five grades were to write a letter to their "father or guardian on some phase of the work of the local Chamber of Commerce. . . ." Other grades were to write themes or give orations on the achievements of the Chamber of Commerce. When union groups and the American Civil Liberties Union protested and demanded a "Union Week" and a "Civil Liberties Week," they were promptly denied.[12]

Across the country Sinclair found local boards dominated by business groups such as the Chamber of Commerce, Kiwanis, and Rotary. Working with these groups was the local American Legion, and together these groups turned schooling into flag-waving 100 percent Americanism and a platform for anti-union and anti-socialist literature. In New York City Sinclair found that teachers were required to take a mayor's pledge of loyalty and that suspected radical teachers were being driven from the schools. Considered as evidence of unpatriotic leanings was the reading of the *New Republic* and the *Nation*. In one instance the Commissioner of Education of New York City went through the textbooks to remove "subversive and unpatriotic" ideas. Across the country Sinclair found the same type of story being told over and over again. In the state of Washington the master of the Washington Progressive Grange related that teachers were refused jobs because they admitted to being members of the Nonpartisan League. The leader of the Grange told Sinclair, "there were grave-yards of radical teachers all over his county. . . ." In some areas liberal boards of education had existed before the patriotic fever of the war forced radicals out of office. In Berkeley, California, a Socialist was elected to the school board in 1911, and in 1913 Socialists had gained control of the Berkeley schools. Sinclair stated that when the war began the Socialist head of the board refused to sign a pledge promising any service to Woodrow Wilson during the war and the Associated Press flashed the news throughout the country. "So the gang," he wrote, "came in waving the stars and stripes, and everything is now back where it was."[13]

Sinclair claimed that social class control also resulted in decisions about schools being made in favor of one social class. It was not accidental from his point of view that the most expensive and best equipped schools were located in wealthier districts in a city while school buildings in poorer districts were firetraps. He also noted that the struggle between vocational and manual education reflected the same social class bias. The schools, he claimed, were being organized to fit the child of the working class into the industrial machine and make him dependent and submissive to its structure. "Modern educators," he wrote, "with their manual training want to use handwork to develop the brains of the child, while the manufacturers want to develop the hands only."[14] And in this statement he reflected his own belief that educational reform was meaningless as long as the schools were dominated by business.

Business control of the school also meant business exploitation. There was not only petty graft involved in school supplies and real estate but, more important, in the link between schooling and the publishing industry. President Atwood of Clark University was only one example. Sinclair found others across the country. Mr. Charles P. Cary, state superintendent of schools in Wisconsin, told him that the American Book Company offered to make him superintendent in a large city and that Ginn and Company tried to buy him during the elections. In Detroit Sinclair claimed the American Book Company controlled the election for the school board. Sinclair reproduced in his book a long letter written by the distinguished educator Charles H. Judd of the University of Chicago describing how the appointment of superintendents in many cities was in the hands of book companies. Judd cited the case of a friend who was invited for an interview for the position of school superintendent in Fort Wayne, Indiana, and was met by the local agent of a book company. In North Dakota Sinclair was told of an agent in the area "whose boast it was that he had placed more school superintendents than any other man in the United States." Sinclair also suggested that book agents controlled the National Education Association.[15]

Upton Sinclair's endless stories of repression and corruption in the American schools cannot all be corroborated. But it does seem accurate to suggest on the basis of his work and the statistics of Scott Nearing and George Counts that there were groups in the United States during this period who viewed business control of the schools as reactionary and repressive. And it is a fact that this feeling of estrangement and concern about plutocratic control led to the attempt to establish an alternative system of schools. Two examples of this effort during the first part of the twentieth century were the Modern School at Stelton, New Jersey, founded as a model for other radical communities in the United States, and the attempt by the labor movement to establish a network of workers' schools and colleges. One of the model labor schools was the Manumit Community School at Pawling, New York.

The Modern School was the product of a wave of concern about the nature of schooling which gripped American radicals following the execution by the Spanish government of the radical educator Francisco Ferrer on charges that he was responsible for a rebellion in Barcelona. The radicals who organized the school did so more out of a sense of frustration with the existing schools than with any definite plan of education. The idea of the school was first born in 1910 at a meeting of the Harlem Liberal Alliance among a mixed group of New York radicals including anarchists, socialists, single taxers, and free thinkers. The leaders of the movement were anarchists and included Emma Goldman and Alexander Berkman. Emma Goldman toured the country during the school's early years raising money for its support. Until 1915 the school was at various locations in New York City and offered the beginnings of a school for young children and courses of lectures for adults on topics ranging from art and Esperanto to sex hygiene and physiology. In 1915 the Modern School established itself at Stelton, New Jersey, where it became a leading center for radical education.[16] The school sent its message to radicals throughout the country in the form of an educational journal called the *Modern School Magazine*, published from 1912 until about 1922. Between 1929 and 1932, Alexis C. Ferm, who assumed joint responsibility with his wife for the principalship of the Modern School in 1920, contributed a regular column on education to the major anarchist journal of the 1920's, *The Road to Freedom*. In 1925 the Modern School Association, having a sense of their purpose of being a model for other radical groups, published a history of their experiment.

As was suggested, the Modern School was born more out of a sentiment than a concrete plan. Harry Kelly, chairman of the first board of management of the school, recalled in 1913, "The Francisco Ferrer Association was 'born of a wave of hysteria'. . . . A deep, underlying protest against the shooting of Ferrer, and a broad, general understanding as to the desirability of a school such as he had started in Spain, were what brought and held us together."[17] The radicals in New York were acquainted with many of Ferrer's ideas about education. Some of his essays had been translated and published in Emma Goldman's magazine *Mother Earth;* and Ferrer's book, *The Origin and Ideals of the Modern School*, was translated and published in New York in 1913. Ferrer's general plan of education emphasized rationalism and the scientific method. One reason for this was a reaction to the Church's domination of the schools in Spain. The heavy emphasis on scientific method and rationalism was not given much attention by American radicals. What American radicals gained from Ferrer's writing was his critique of the nature of modern schooling.

Ferrer's primary argument was that the modern drive for public schooling born in the nineteenth century was not the product of a desire to free men but the result of the needs of industrialized countries for trained workers so those countries could remain competitive in the international marketplace. Ferrer's critique came to the attention of American radicals in the form of an article published in 1909 in *Mother Earth*. He directly connected the power of the state and industry to that of the school. For Ferrer control of the school system was one of the main sources of social power. Ferrer wrote, "Governments have ever been careful to hold a high hand over the education of the people. They know, better than anyone else, that their power is based almost entirely on the school. Hence, they monopolize it more and more." He argued that in the past governments could maintain control of the people by keeping them in a state of ignorance. But with international industrial competition this had become impossible. Everyone's cry in the nineteenth century had become: "For and by the School." The current popularity of the school, Ferrer argued, rested on its ability to be used as an instrument of control by the state and of domination by industry. Ferrer claimed that "the organization of the school, far from spreading the ideal which we imagined, has made education the most powerful means of enslavement in the hands of governing powers to-day." The teachers within the organization of the school, according to Ferrer, could effect little change because the power of the organization of the school constrained them into obedience. Ferrer argued that those who established public schools had one desire and that was that "Children must be accustomed to obey, to believe, to think, according to the social dogmas which govern us." For Ferrer the answer was not reform of the school but the creation of a different type of institution. He wrote that public school advocates "never wanted the uplift of the individual, but his enslavement; and it is perfectly useless to hope for anything from the school of to-day."[18]

The people connected with the Modern School at Stelton leveled the same type of critique at the public schools in the United States. Whether this was the result of Ferrer's influence or just a product of conditions within the United States would be difficult to determine. For instance, Harry Kelly, chairman of the first board of management of the school, wrote ten years after its establishment in Stelton, "We saw then and we see now, that the public school system is a powerful instrument for the perpetuation of the present social order with all its injustice and inequality . . . and that, quite naturally, whatever is likely to disturb the existing arrangement is regarded unfavorably by those in control of the public schools." Kelly, with arguments that paralleled those of Ferrer, claimed that the primary purpose of the public schools was the perpetuation of authority within society. "From the moment the child enters the public school he is trained to submit to authority, to do the will of others as a matter of course, with the result that habits of mind are formed which in adult life are all to the advantage of the ruling class." Schools destroyed initiative and individuality "except in the narrow fields where these qualities can increase the efficiency of the capitalist machine."[19]

The general feeling of radicals who gathered around Stelton was that the development of an alternative system of education was to be the first step toward any major social change. They became convinced that radical movements of the past had been frustrated because the power and meaning of schooling had been unrealized. James H. Dick, one of the most dedicated teachers at Stelton, wrote in 1929, "The strangest phenomenon of all is the fact that the vast majority of radicals of all shades of opinion have some sort of devout feeling for this one governmental institution, having some vague notion that education is above propaganda."[20] Alexis Ferm, the co-principal of the Modern School, argued that when workers had originally struggled for the establishment of schools, they were not thinking of schools in terms of education but as a means of equalizing opportunities. Consequently when workers won their schools, they thought they had solved the problem for their children. The workers failed because they turned schools over to the authorities and retained no control over the actual educational process. Ferm wrote that the workers forgot "that the authorities were the very exploiters of labor against whose encroachments upon their liberties the workers were organized to defend themselves." Workers' children, by being well schooled, failed to understand the reactionary role of the school and the necessity for questioning its control.[21]

The result of failing to understand the role of the school was the continued inability of the working class adequately to question the existing social order. The schools conditioned for authority and turned out workers completely obedient to the needs of capitalism. James Dick argued that one of the powerful persuaders and controlling devices of the school was the promise of economic prosperity. The worker was convinced that the school was the ladder for his child's economic advancement. Dick wrote that for the worker, "The seductive atmosphere of 'prosperity' is too much for him, and the lethal chambers of a governmental scholastic career for his child is the real solution to his salvation."[22] The irony, of course, was that as the schools promised, they also controlled. The school represented the contradictions inherent in twentieth century institutions.

What radicals failed to realize, according to the Stelton group, was that it was not just the propaganda used in the public schools but the very process of schooling that was important. Alexis Ferm argued that the process of public schooling assumed that a course of study should be established for the student's "own good." This meant the student was not given a choice but depended on the advice of authorities. "It is considered," Ferm wrote, "that his choice would not be any good anyhow and that he should be taught to accept things without question, to admire our captains of industry, our Presidents who bring us prosperity, our army and navy and our religions."[23] What students really learned in school, Ferm claimed, were the rules and techniques for getting through school. These rules and techniques were not necessarily related to the process of real learning and critical thinking. Radical parents were foolish to think they could handle the problem of social attitudes in the home by exposing their children to radical propaganda. This did not counteract the effect of the method of thinking taught by the process of schooling.

Alexis Ferm speculated that some day it might be demonstrated that a genuine education could not be a public affair. "It may come to us," Ferm wrote, "that schools in order to be educational centers will have to be local affairs sponsored by the groups that want to use them."[24] This, of course, was precisely how the Modern School was organized. The Modern School was to be a model for the type of education center the radicals were to create as an alternative to the existing system. The school embodied a style and method of approaching the child rather than a concrete blueprint. This style was mainly the result of the work of Elizabeth Ferm, who attempted to give meaning to the ideas of freedom and self-determination in education. She was born in 1857 in Illinois and her career included a long list of radical activities. In the 1880's she was working for Henry George's Anti-Poverty Society and was active in the Woman's Suffrage Movement. During this period she attended a training school for kindergartners in Montreal, and during the 1890's she become actively involved in kindergarten work in New York, where she met other radical groups who eventually involved her in the Modern School.[25] During the early part of the twentieth century she was contributing educational articles to the anarchist journal *Mother Earth*.[26] Elizabeth Ferms' work at Stelton was a combination of her early training in kindergarten work and her belief in self-determination and freedom. One of her main concerns was that teachers would confuse self-determination for the child with passivity for the educator. The distinction between the pedagogue and educator, she always claimed, was the difference between the person who wanted to make the child into something and the person who wanted to help the child determine what he wanted to be. The educator was the active and not passive participant in the child's quest for self-expression. The role of the educator was to give meaning to that self-expression. In this manner the individual would learn to be his own authority and realize the usefulness and necessity of help from others.

The Modern School at Stelton had contact with the growing wave of labor schools and colleges and were being established in reaction to what was considered business domination of the schools. In 1917 both Harry Kelly and James Dick tried to begin a labor college at Stelton. While it never materialized, the Stelton group never lost contact with the movement and frequently invited one of the leading exponents of labor colleges, A. J. Muste, to its annual meetings. All the radical groups and labor leaders seemed to be connected through a fine web of publications and contacts during the early part of the century. While one cannot measure the influence of Stelton on the development of labor schools and colleges, it is clear they shared a common view, that the public schools were not functioning in the interests of the working class.

In some ways the labor colleges and schools had a more important impact than radical schools like the Modern School. Some educators associated with the established public school systems viewed with serious concern the growing development of labor schools. George Counts' *The Social Composition of Boards of Education* was written within the framework of labor's attitudes toward the school. In 1925, Ernest H. Lindley, the Chancellor of the University of Kansas, in his presidential address at the annual convention of the National Association of State Universities warned, "Many leaders in the ranks of organized labor believe the state universities, as well as private foundations, are under the domination of special interests." Lindley called upon the convention to rid the universities of undemocratic practices and establish courses and train teachers to meet labor's needs. He emphasized that "the active movement for the establishment of independent labor colleges in the United States, where there exist state-supported institutions in nearly every commonwealth, is an impressive phenomenon."[27] How widespread the concern about labor schools was among professional educators would be difficult to measure. On the one hand many educators came to advocate teachers' unions as one way of combating the control by special interests. On the other hand, most of those involved in the development of labor schools complained of continued resistance and reaction by the public schools.

One example of bitter complaint was described by James H. Maurer, one of the leaders of the labor education movement in Pennsylvania. Writing in the *Nation* in 1922, he recalled how in one Pennsylvania town the public school refused to provide a classroom for labor education classes. The board of education finally agreed to provide a room if the labor group would accept a teacher appointed by the board. Maurer noted that the idea of adult working-class students electing their own teacher was too radical for the board. "Yet," Maurer wrote, "in the same schools the chamber of commerce, the American Legion, and similar organizations can send representatives at any time to talk to the students on any subject. Even a junior chamber of commerce has been organized in the high school." Maurer believed it was crucial for the modern labor movement to establish a mechanism to transmit information and describe methods of handling modern social problems. Why not use existing educational institutions? Maurer wrote, "The suggestion of a college or university reminds the active unionist of the persecution of professors for showing too much interest in the welfare of the masses, and brings to his mind pictures of college students as strike-breakers." In the public schools it was even more difficult to imagine having labor's point of view presented. For example, Maurer stated, in Pennsylvania the American Federation of Teachers had been outlawed. Given this situation the only hope was the establishment of an alternative network of schools and colleges. Maurer reported that the movement for labor education had been growing rapidly and that at a conference on labor education in 1921 reports were heard from twenty-five labor schools and colleges in the United States.[28]

In September 1924, seventy representatives of labor and education journeyed to Pawling, New York, for a two-day conference and to participate in the founding of Manumit School. A writer in the *Nation* referred to the occasion as symbolizing "an alliance of progressive labor and progressive education." The term progressive in this particular case did not have the same meaning as it had in the ideology which had shaped the public school during the early part of the century. Progressive as used by these labor leaders and educators connoted a rebellion against the processes within the public schools that were shaping individuals for the needs of the corporate state. This changing use of the term progressive would later lead educational historians into placing these two movements within the same framework. The founders of Manumit, quite distinctly and in many ways as a statement of rebellion against the ideology of the American school, established Manumit "primarily for the children of workers." The writer in the *Nation* stated, "What Manumit stands for, in its relation to labor, is the free, untrammeled inquiry of the child's mind, when he displays a readiness for it, into the basic functions, problems, and ideals of the toilers, which in the public schools are deliberately withheld from his intellectual and emotional experience."[29]

Manumit was established as a boarding school for children of workers between the ages of 9 and 14. It was located on a 177-acre farm with cattle, hills, and a stream for swimming and fishing. One of the papers of intention presented by the new faculty at the founding meeting of the school called it a community school to affirm Dewey's belief that education comes through life. "The community life of our school," the paper stated, "is the socialized incarnation of our belief in industrial democracy." This statement reflected the strange career of John Dewey's ideas. The public schools could point to Dewey's concept of community and use it as a justification for socialization into an interdependent corporate state. Radicals reading Dewey took the idea of community and translated it into industrial democracy.[30]

Manumit was planned as a boarding school to give real meaning to the concept of community. Students were to be self-governing and learn the principles of community through the day-to-day experiences at Manumit. Work and organization within the community were all organized on the principle of democratic control by the students. The statement of purposes of Manumit reflected a hope that by having a 24-hour community one could avoid the artificial contrivances that the public school had to use to promote a spirit of community. This would eliminate a concern about whether an individual spent too much or too little time working with others. Group action would become a natural product of the work of the community.

By 1927 Manumit had thirty-eight students and six teachers with each member of the community having one vote. In terms of organization it had many of the same features as the George Junior Republic, but in terms of spirit it functioned in a completely different manner. One example was related by a teacher in an article in the *Nation*. On one cold winter morning the children found they were without breakfast. A student had refused to cook because the supper squad had failed to wash the dishes the previous evening. The supper squad had not done the dishes because one of its members went on strike, claiming he had been assigned the duty for a long period of time. Other members of the community had washed the dishes, but this did not satisfy the cook. She claimed that if the supper squad did not wash the dishes they were not officially done. The community met as a group and there was a heated debate between the strict constitutionalists led by the cook and others who wanted to eat. Finally in the heat of the debate a motion was presented and adopted that holding up breakfast was out of order and the community adjourned to have breakfast.[31]

The teacher who reported the above incident considered it as one example of how children can learn to function in a collective and democratic manner. She saw the function of Manumit in the same terms as the group at Stelton. It was to be a model and example for the establishment of other labor schools. It planned to accomplish this aim without the artificial and controlling devices of the public schools. She wrote, "It hopes to serve as a laboratory or demonstration school of the labor movement, where creative activity can be tried out in an environment that furnishes fundamental life processes rather than artificially devised schemes as project material, and where it can be applied to a typical group of public-school children."[32]

Alternative schools were not the only options available to the labor movement. One of these options was to direct organized pressures toward local school districts to implement a more liberal educational policy. In 1922 the American Federation of Labor in a pamphlet entitled *Education for All* called upon central labor bodies to fight for representation on school boards. It was hoped that if organized labor began to win control of school boards there would be increased use of adult education for labor purposes and liberally conducted courses. The American Federation of Labor warned, "If the public school system does not show willingness to co-operate in offering appropriate courses and type of instruction, the central labor body should organize such classes with as much co-operation from the public schools as may be obtained."[33] Labor's attempt to gain control of local school boards became an important issue during the Depression, when many labor organizations actually did come to dominate boards of education in some areas.

The other option was teachers' unions. These were viewed as not only a means for assuring academic freedom in the schools but also as a vehicle for getting a more liberal ideology into the schools. For instance, Upton Sinclair firmly believed that the only salvation for American education was in teachers' gaining power through organized unions and the use of the strike. He assumed that professional control of the schools would mean the end of business control for profit and propaganda. George Counts was to voice a similar belief in the 1930's in his famous *Dare the School Build a New Social Order.* Disillusionment would set in later when it appeared that even with a certain amount of academic freedom, teachers still tended to follow a conservative ideology.

The failure to establish a viable and extensive alternative system of education reflected the shallowness of the radical criticism of the public schools. Most of the criticism of the labor movement was directed toward the problem of control and antilabor ideology. By the end of the Depression and certainly by the end of World War II most labor groups and businessmen accepted the corporate ideology of Samuel Gompers and the National Civil Federation. Collective bargaining by unions was considered as part of the democratic process. Labor's discontent with the schools dissipated when this argument became part of the schools' definition of democracy. As more and more pro-labor material entered the schools, the urge for an alternative system of labor schools diminished.

Despite the failure to adopt a lasting alternative system of schools the discontent continued until the avalanche of free schools in the 1960's and 1970's. The failure and discontent resulted from the inability of radicals to realize that the problem was not the ideology of schooling nor the methods. The problem was the process of schooling. The significance of the American high school was not the content of its curriculum but the social process of clubs, student government, differentiation, and all the extra-curricular activities which socialized the individual for the benefit of the corporate state.

CHAPTER EIGHT

THE MEANING OF SCHOOLING IN
THE TWENTIETH CENTURY

I

The school is and has been an instrument of social, economic, and political control. It is an institution which consciously plans to turn people into something. Within this framework the school must be viewed as an instrument of power. It creates an institutional relationship which gives power to a social group to consciously shape the personality and goals of an entire generation. Those in control could be all adults, businessmen, teachers, professional bureaucrats, or politicians. Since 1900 the power of schooling has tended to be in the hands of businessmen, political leaders, and professional educators who have been instrumental in the development of the modern corporate state.

To understand the power of the school one must not confuse the learning of traditional academic subjects with the process of schooling. The most important feature of the school in the twentieth century is its role as the major institution for socialization. The process of socialization includes the individual's relationship with the institution of the school, the quality of his relationships with his peers, and his place in the social structure of the school. The major changes in education during this century were the result of a concern for the type and direction of socialization. Grades, assemblies, differentiation of courses of study, extra-curricular activities, and the school as a community were all part of the discussion about refining the nature and power of the school as a controlling institution.

Two important distinctions must be made about the issue of control in education. First, there is the question of who controls the educational process. This question leads to a discussion of the role of boards of education, of professional teacher organizations, and of the relationship between local, state, and Federal government involvement in education.[1] During the late nineteenth and the early twentieth centuries this debate resulted in the centralization of urban school boards and the concentration of power in the hands of the business and professional community. During the last half of the twentieth century the debate shifted to a demand for community control of the schools. In this case civil rights groups discovered they were without power to control their schools because of the conscious effort by groups at the beginning of the century to concentrate control of the schools in the hands of the business and social elite.

The second question is much more subtle and deals with the type or nature of power that the process of schooling prepares the individual to accept. For instance, radicals during the early part of the century claimed that schooling prepared the individual to accept the control of business and industry. It was claimed that the habits of obedience and industriousness learned in the school resulted in the unquestioning acceptance of and obedience to capitalist leaders. On the other hand, progressive leaders saw themselves creating an educational system which would prepare the individual to accept a system of co-operation and control by a meritocracy.

Another example of the process of schooling as preparation for control is that of the segregated schools of the South. The socialization that was to result from segregated schools was designed to perpetuate a caste system and assure the domination of one racial group over another. The impact of these schools was not so much in what was taught but that the institutions for socialization were segregated and those provided for Black students were of an inferior quality. This system was not accidental but the result of conscious plans by industrial leaders to segregate the Black population and educate them as an inexpensive labor force for the new industrial South.[2]

In the case of the segregated schools in the South during the first half of the century the socialization process was directed toward both the acceptance of the dominant controlling power of the white race and also the acceptance of a caste-oriented social structure. This example emphasizes one of the important results of the socialization process of schooling. Schools tend to reinforce and strengthen existing social structures and social stratification. The rhetoric of schooling has always suggested that schools break down social class lines. By the 1940's sociologists began to argue that rather than breaking down social class lines schools actually were strengthening them by schooling people into their social positions.

One of the first important studies to focus on this issue was conducted by a team of sociologists in a small town in Indiana in the 1940's. The study, titled *Elmstown's Youth,* explored the relationship between social classes and adolescent life. One of the focuses of the study, of course, was the local high school. The sociologists found that the process of differentiation in the comprehensive high school reflected the social classes within the community. The community was divided into five social classes, with those with established wealth in the first group, important business and professional leaders in the second group, small businessmen and minor professionals in the third group, millworkers and white-collar clerks in the fourth group, and the lowest social class included unskilled and semiskilled workers and the unemployed. These social class divisions were reflected in the differentiated courses of studies offered in the high school. Adolescents from social classes one, two, and three dominated the college preparatory track; the general track drew the majority of its students from social classes three and four; and the commercial track received students primarily from the two lowest social classes.

The comprehensive high school attended by Elmstown's

youth strengthened the social stratification of the community. The great cry of progressive reformers for differentiated studies and for "meeting individual needs" had resulted in the school's perpetuating social class lines and schooling people into their social places. School reformers, of course, had been aware of this possibility and attempted to overcome it through the social mixing of extra-curricular activities. The irony was that in Elmstown this failed. In Elmstown it was found that adolescent participation in extra-curricular activities varied according to social classes. In terms of participation in at least one extra-curricular activity it was found in Elmstown that adolescents from social classes one and two had 100 percent participation, social class three had 75.3 percent, class four 57.4 percent, and in social class five only 27 percent participated in extra-curricular activities.[3]

Schooling not only prepares for the acceptance of control by dominant elites and social structures but also can create a dependence on institutions and expertise. The fact that the school assumes responsibility for the whole child brings all human actions under the expertise of the school and subjects them to the criteria of schooling. One learns in school that thinking, acting, dressing, playing, and creating can be placed on a linear scale and ranked and graded according to value. The school teaches sex, driving, problems in leisure time, and a whole host of related subjects. The concept of school preparing one for "worthy use of leisure time" is an example of this situation. This concept suggests that certain leisure time activities are more worthwhile than others and that if one wishes to use his leisure time "properly," he goes to an expert. The expert establishes the standard of "proper" leisure, then trains the individual to enjoy life.

This form of institutional dependence can potentially freeze and deaden all human activity. It is not beyond the realm of possibility, for instance, that sometime in the future people will not engage in sexual acts until "properly" taught the most valuable response and the most scientific method. It seems possible that in the current discussions in geriatrics there will develop techniques to help people die "properly." Death education and sex education will probably become important elements in our educational system if current practices continue.

A manifestation of this institutional dependence is the current trend in educational institutions to extend credit to a wide variety of activities. Institutions are giving credit for vacations, social work, and community activities. This brings not only the whole child into the school but also all of his activities. In the future, individuals might only participate in activities if the school will approve them and give them credit. As a student once suggested to me, people will start demanding three hours credit for being born.

Dependence upon institutions and expertise represents a form of alienation which goes far beyond anything suggested by Karl Marx in the nineteenth century. One of Ivan Illich's arguments regarding the necessity of deschooling society focuses on this concept of alienation.[4] What the school accomplishes is the alienation of man's ability to act or create his own social being. In the nineteenth century Karl Marx argued that the product of man's activity represented an objectification of self. What men produced through their activity was a reflection and objectification which gave men an awareness of self and related them to society. Alienation in this context meant that the product of labor became foreign or alien to the individual. This condition resulted from a combination of new industrial organizations and capitalism. Marx defined alienation as, "First, that the work is external to the worker, that it is not part of his nature; and that, consequently, he does not fulfill himself in his work but denies himself, has a feeling of misery rather than well being. . . . It is not the satisfaction of a need, but only a means for satisfying other needs."[5] The alienation of the product of man's activity resulted in the alienation of men. Since men could not relate to the product of their activity, they could not relate to the social use of that product. For Marx it was the social use of the products of men that held men together in a meaningful society. Marx wrote, "A direct consequence of the alienation of man from the product of his labor, from his life activity, and from his species life is that man is alienated from other men. When man confronts himself, he also confronts other men."[6]

The triumph of the school in the twentieth century has resulted in the expansion of this concept of alienation. Technology and state capitalism still make work meaningless to the individual and create a condition of alienation from the product of labor. The school increases this alienation by making alien the very ability of the individual to act or create. In school the ability to act is no longer an individual matter but is turned over to experts who grade, rank, and prescribe. Activity, itself, no longer belongs to the individual but to the institution and its experts. In the nineteenth century man lost the product of his labor; in the twentieth century man lost his will.

The themes of control, social stratification, and institutional dependency are all finely interwoven. Certainly those in control of the schools would like to see a reproduction of the social structure which allowed them to control the schools. In other words, the schools by their very nature tend to be conservative and provide a vehicle for the continuation of existing social stratification. In the same manner, existing institutions and experts tend to be supportive of existing social structures and power relationships. It is certainly to the advantage of those who dominate a society to create a dependence upon those institutions and experts which reflect their power. In fact, this might be one of the most controlling factors of the schools.

II

The power of the school cannot be explained simply in terms of human control. One of the dominant themes of schooling in the twentieth century is adjustment to the changing nature of technology. A great deal of educational rhetoric during the early part of the twentieth century was directed toward alienation and the perceived destruction of community caused by technology. Certainly much of Dewey's work centered on this problem. After World War II there was not only fear about the domination of technology but also a feeling that automation and mass media were having an effect upon the individual different from that of previous industrial organizations. Technology became either a monster enslaving man or the creator of a utopian world village.

After World War II the picture of the isolated worker on the assembly line and the citizen lacking social awareness was no longer an accurate representation of society. The automated industrial systems of the post–World War II era put the worker in charge of a total industrial process. He was not isolated by technology but forced by the interdependence of the automated process into an awareness of the whole system. Radio, movies, and especially television provided a sense of community and social awareness felt lacking at the beginning of the century. By the 1960's children were entering school with a high degree of political and social sophistication. The mass media bombarded the child with a wide variety of information placed in different cultural contexts. Technology and mass media made many aspects of the socialization programs obsolete. Teaching a child about the workings of democracy through student government became useless and sometimes silly when the child consumed the political satire of *Mad* magazine after school hours.

The man who has viewed these changes favorably is Marshall McLuhan. In a sense Marshall McLuhan has updated John Dewey. Dewey had argued at the beginning of the century that the school had to constantly adapt to changing social conditions. McLuhan feels the social conditions to which Dewey was reacting no longer exist. When Dewey was at the University of Chicago at the turn of the century, the gap he perceived that had to be filled in society was the creation of a sense of community. The factories and cities were failing in this respect, and the schools had to fill this unique role. To Dewey, education for meeting social needs centered on developing a spirit of community. McLuhan would agree that a sense of common purpose was lacking during the early stages of industrial development, but, since World War II, technology has tended to unify man's experiences rather than fragment them. McLuhan's world village through media and automation, if correct, would replace the school as the center of the community.

McLuhan's basic thesis is that technology teaches men how to organize their experiences and also organizes the type of experiences men will have. For instance, the combination of phonetic alphabet and the development of printing, the two most important developments in the Western world according to McLuhan, organized experiences into a linear, sequential line. The printed page not only presented the experiences of the world to man in a particular manner but also conditioned man to organize his experiences to conform to the pattern of the printed sentence. The effect of the phonetic alphabet has been to make Western man expect the world to act in a linear or rational manner. McLuhan suggests this is what differentiates the Eastern from Western man. McLuhan also believes that print developed a strong sense of "detachment and noninvolvement—the power to act without reacting."[7] Receiving experiences through the printed page allowed the individual to remain personally uninvolved. It also abstracted the experience from a real, total context and created the attitude that eventually was called scientific objectivity. Lofty detachment and disinterest became criteria for a good scientific attitude. The printed phonetic alphabet therefore conditioned man to organize his experiences in a particular manner and to expect the world to act in a certain fashion. McLuhan also believes the printed book is an example of how technology works to organize the type of world man experiences. Print provides the tools to control large organizations and link larger numbers of people together through common reading. A national mass literature becomes possible with a press and, consequently, a growth of nationalistic spirit. Nationalism and large organizations create entirely different forms of social relationships.

It is doubtful that Dewey would have agreed with McLuhan's interpretation of the effect of the Gutenberg revolution, but he would have agreed with his interpretation of the consequences of early industrialism. Dewey and McLuhan share a belief in the importance of the effect of technological development on the social relationships of man. Like Karl Marx and Dewey, McLuhan argues that industrialism bred a sense of antisocial individualism which was destructive to both the man and the community. The worker on the assembly line encountered a fragmented world which lacked a sense of wholeness and continuity. Whereas Marx wanted to change this situation by changing the economic structure and Dewey wanted to use the schools, McLuhan sees technology as providing its own cure. McLuhan writes, "The result of electric speed-up in industry at large is the creation of intense sensitivity to the interrelation and interprocess of the whole. . . ."[8] The worker today pushes one button and rapidly completes one total process. According to McLuhan experience in an automated factory is total and not fragmentary.

The major inference McLuhan draws from the technological developments of the post-World War II era completely contradicts earlier fears of technology. McLuhan predicts the evolvement of a global village, which he feels will be the result of television and automation. Both make the individual aware of social interdependence and give him a sense of involvement. Print and the assembly line fragmented and abstracted experience, while the new media and technology integrate and personalize experience. If McLuhan is correct, then Dewey's dictum that the school must become a community has to be updated. The development of a community would now be the result of technology and not of the public schools. McLuhan's new village life would be one of total involvement and living for the here and now. "The TV child," McLuhan writes, "cannot see ahead because he wants involvement, and he cannot accept a fragmentary and merely visualized goal or destiny in learning or life."[9] The image of McLuhan's TV child is the complete opposite of the fragmented industrial cipher of the nineteenth century.

McLuhan's vision of a global village contains a degree of utopian optimism not necessarily supported by technological developments. The unity being created by automation and media might mean enslavement, not liberation. The heavy stress upon unity and cooperation at the beginning of the twentieth century was the result of fear about the direction of the new industrial forces. Henry Adams reflected the feelings of his generation when he proposed in his autobiography a theory of history that saw civilization moving from unity to chaos.[10] Fifty years later fear of chaos shifted to fear of the organizational capabilities of computers. Feedback and computer storage banks made large tightly knit organizations feasible. The problem was not in being lost or destroyed in the chaos of development but being enslaved by technological organization. McLuhan is probably right that there is now a greater sense of unity and involvement, but this could be de-humanizing.

The possibility of human enslavement to technology has been suggested by the French sociologist Jacques Ellul. He argues that technology was originally intended to be a buffer between man and nature. It has functioned so well that man has lost all contact with his original needs. Technology now dominates the goals and aspirations of man. Human labor at one time was directed toward goals defined by human necessity. According to Ellul technology now defines the goals of human action and these goals are not necessarily related to human needs. The goals of the technological system are directed toward its perpetuation and expansion. Consumption and production became the dominating forces. The technological system does not work for the benefit of man but for its own benefit. Man becomes, to use Ellul's term, a "thing" to be controlled for the benefit of the system. Ellul, unlike McLuhan, is not optimistic about the use and development of mass media. Media just provides further methods for enslavement. Advertising in mass media manipulates tastes and creates desires that are not related to human needs but to the productive needs of technology. Ellul does perceive a certain irony in the situation. As psychological controls become more refined it may be possible to "feel" happy no matter what the physical conditions. The man of the future might be capable of happiness under the worst deprivations. Ellul suggests that this might be accomplished through direct control of the nervous system. This would mean that one could be happy without the products and comforts considered necessary by the technological system. "The last meager motive we could possibly ascribe to the technical adventure," Ellul writes, "thus vanishes into thin air through the very existence of technique itself."[11]

Ellul argues that "progressive" education's emphasis on social adjustment made the other goals of liberation and individualized instruction meaningless. Once the school assumed responsibility for the total development of the child, it became responsible for assuring that the child was shaped to fit into society. This occurred because personality problems were defined in terms of social relationships. Ellul writes, "Opposition to society, the lack of social adaptation, produces serious personality difficulties which lead to the loss of psychic equilibrium."[12] The most important factor in education therefore became social adjustment to restore the psychic balance. Ellul points out that this social adaptation was to a society that was neither perfect nor ideal. In fact as society becomes more technological and totalitarian, the problems of adaptation become more and more difficult. This leads to the further development of more refined techniques of adjustment and makes socialization even more necessary. Therefore as technology advances, the burden of making people "happy" becomes more and more the responsibility of education. Paradoxically this creates the impression that education is becoming more humanistic. Ellul suggests, "What looks like the apex of humanism is in fact the pinnacle of human submission: children are educated to become precisely what society expects of them. They must have social consciences that allow them to strive for the same ends as society sets for itself."[13]

The link established between education and technological suppression makes vocational guidance one of the great villains. Basing his argument on the work of French Marxist Pierre Naville, Ellul suggests that there are no such things as natural aptitudes. Vocational guidance does not in fact discover natural aptitudes but " 'discovers' in the individuals examined precisely the aptitudes which are essential to the needs of the capitalist system." Ellul points out the interesting situation that would occur if vocational guidance really did discover natural aptitudes and these aptitudes were developed and utilized.

The result would be that the entire economy would be based on these aptitudes. The situation might occur where vocational guidance could discover no mechanics. This would mean that all machine shops would have to be closed. The same thing would be true of other occupations. Ellul correctly states that this system of guidance would be extremely logical if we were concerned with the primacy of the individual. "The obvious impossibility of such a system," Ellul writes, "demonstrates that it is senseless to apply the rule of the primacy of the individual and that vocational guidance cannot be isolated from the other techniques."[14]

Besides the fact that vocational guidance was originally intended to be a part of the economic system, inevitably it must become, according to Ellul, a tool of the technological system. Vocational guidance, like education in general, suffers from a benevolent desire to help. The child's character must be developed to the fullest and a rewarding place found for him in society. This benevolent goal leads to molding individual character to fit it into a particular slot in the system. The educator and vocational guidance counselor cannot change the system, consequently they change the individual. If they did not adapt the individual to the system, they in fact would be creating maladjusted citizens who might suffer and cause dissension in the society. This result would be considered a failure in developing personality and making people happy. The rhetoric of vocational guidance and education therefore becomes self-defeating. Benevolent help and individualization mean in the end adapting the individual to the technological system by making its goals and needs a total part of the personality.

There is very little difference between what Ellul sees as the consequences of modern education and the goals of educational reformers at the beginning of the twentieth century. The real differences lie in their attitudes toward technology. For Ellul technology is a growing monster which is slowly and inevitably enslaving and dehumanizing mankind. On the other hand, early twentieth century educators welcomed the adjustment of humanity to the technological processes. Far from being a mechanism for enslavement, it promised happiness and fulfillment. It is precisely Croly's definition of individualism to which Ellul is objecting. Croly's idea of individualism, based on a specialized task in the system, would be rejected by Ellul because it makes man a tool of technology rather than allowing him to be directed by his own human needs. To a certain extent Ellul is right. Educators, industrialists, and politicians did talk about human beings as if they were things to be readied for the industrial process. The population became a great natural resource to be trained and protected for the greater industrial development of the country.

Ellul and McLuhan provide different ways of viewing the effect of technology on modern schooling. Both assume a deterministic relationship between technology and schooling. For McLuhan technology determines the style of all of our institutions. From his standpoint the school is no longer a requirement of technology. The alienated community of early industrialism has been replaced by a tribal community of mass media and automation. Socialization within the school is irrelevant to the needs of the modern world. On the other hand, Ellul sees the continued integration of educational processes and technological development. The school becomes a source of power for the technological machine.

One of the weaknesses of both Ellul and McLuhan is the failure to link the structure and meaning of technology to economic and social class interests. It is difficult to accept a completely deterministic model of technology. The development of technology has been the result of an interplay of human desires and industrial development. Men have not been completely independent of the forces of technology, nor have they been completely the slaves of those forces. Ellul is probably correct about the adjustment of the schools to fulfill the needs of the new industrial state. What he fails to emphasize is that the new technology operated for the benefit of certain groups within the state. As the schools adjusted to the demands of technology, they also adjusted to the needs of those who controlled technology. Technology, social stratification, institutional dependence, and social control are all interrelated.

III

One of the sources of power of the school in the twentieth century has been the belief that education is the most humane and democratic form of social control. Giving the schools this responsibility provides them with even greater power to shape and mold lives. From the time of Horace Mann education as social control was to reform society by training men to be socially good. As has been shown this type of thinking led to the encompassing of more and more of the social life of the child in the school. The reduction of contacts with the rest of the environment was to result in a well controlled and moral education.

Education for social control was certainly the result of a humanitarian and benevolent attitude. The conditions in the slums were deplorable and probably did cause juvenile delinquency and crime. But the attitude of saving the child from his own world did carry with it a feeling of moral superiority. The slum child was to be saved from his world and that of his parents by the imposition of a particular style of middle class life. Black parents in later years were to react to precisely this form of imposition. The humanitarianism of social control was therefore accompanied by an attitude that negated any broad concept of freedom. While there was a belief that activity and participation were to be an integral part of education, this did not mean activity or participation were to be directed toward any goal selected by the students. William Heard Kilpatrick's method claimed that it allowed the student to choose ends but then always tempered this claim with a discussion about choosing socially valuable ends. It was perfectly true that under older nineteenth century methods there was less freedom for the student, but no one ever claimed that they were free. After the educational changes of the early part of the twentieth century, freedom became a popular way of describing educational activity. As the school expanded and gained a greater role in social control there was more and more talk about allowing freedom in the school. Looking at the phenomenon in retrospect it appears that calling the activities of the classroom "free" was one way of avoiding the fact that less and less of the child's life was free.

At least the student in the classroom in the nineteenth century knew that he was not free and that freedom was something one exercised outside of institutional controls. Whether the nineteenth century man was free in any existential sense is a moot question. It can be argued that at least the educational environment did not necessarily hinder his freedom to act later in life. By freedom in this case is meant the ability to choose goals consistent with your own personal desires and the ability to fulfill those goals. The child in the socialized classroom learned that freedom was working to accomplish group and institutional goals. Any concern about personal desires was a reflection of "selfish" individualism. The child also learned that freedom was something exercised within the context of institutional controls. The socialized classroom taught one how to act in a corporation but not as a free man; of course, neither did the more traditional school. The difference was that in the socialized school the student was told that he was free, and, consequently, there was the danger that he might think that this was the only meaning of freedom.

Education as social control therefore might appear on the surface as a more democratic form of control because of its claim to both internal and external freedom. In actuality democracy as it pertains to personal choice becomes an illusion if freedom is reduced to acting in terms of social needs. Children are taught to feel free even though their lives are being directed by institutional forces. A well-functioning democracy becomes more possible in a society of aware slaves. At least they would know that freedom involves some form of individual direction.

Another magical word in education, one more widely used than freedom, has been individualism. Throughout the writings of the social educators appears the golden term, individualization. Meeting individual needs and providing for individual differences were two phrases that were sorely overworked. It was believed that as long as education individualized instruction, it maintained some contact with democracy. At times individualization meant using individual methods to assure that every student achieved the same goal. This definition was used in reference to both character training and academic subjects. If one wanted children to be thrifty or learn algebra, one used different methods with each child. Somehow this form of individualization was to be democratic. Another use of individualization referred to training the individual for a specialized slot in the social system. Individual differences were in this case defined in terms of one's particular contribution to the organization. The suggestion was not made that individualization might mean the development of an individual life style.

It might be the case that education as social control cannot allow for the development of individual life styles. To even assume that education can effectively reform society is to assume that there is a "good way to live." This means that character molding in the school will be directed toward one particular goal defined in terms of the good society. As Ellul pointed out, this means that the individual's personality is developed not for itself but for what it can do to improve society. Education for social control is organized, after all, in terms of controlling and improving society. The goals of individual development must be consistent with this end.

The argument can also be made that institutional environments—in this case the schools—are not conducive to the development of a variety of life styles. The very functioning of these environments depends on social order. A school cannot function if disruptive personalities cause a breakdown of institutional order. Running and shouting in school corridors, for instance, would make communication in the classroom impossible. The only type of personality the school can support and approve is one that fits smoothly into the institutional organization. This means that for the school to survive it can nurture and develop only those behaviors which do not conflict with its institutional needs. The extension of compulsory education laws and the increased amount of time, both in terms of hours each day and in added years, has brought a greater part of the population under institutional controls. If the schools, because of their structure, nurture only one type of personality, this would mean the development of one dominant life style. Of course, in terms of the well-functioning society no objection to this condition need be raised. The type of personality needed in the school is the same as that needed in the corporation.

Education as social control therefore is not democratic if democracy means freedom to choose one's own goals and the opportunity to develop one's own life style. The use of education to solve social problems often results in overlooking the social conditions that originally caused the problems. As the techniques of education develop, there is the danger that the student can be taught to feel free and happy under any conditions. As Ellul suggests, human history might end with man feeling contented and happy as the world crumbles, starvation runs rampant, and political institutions collapse.

Education can become anti-democratic when social control and the rhetoric of permissiveness blend. Erich Fromm in the introduction to *Summerhill* argues that the transition from the discipline of the nineteenth century to the permissiveness of the twentieth has resulted not in the rejection of authoritarianism but in a shift from overt authority to anonymous authority. The overt authority of the nineteenth century frankly told the student that he would be punished. According to Fromm anonymous authority tends to hide the force that is being used. He writes, "Here, the sanction for disobedience is not corporal punishment, but the suffering face of the parent, or what is worse, conveying the feeling of not being 'adjusted,' of not acting as the crowd acts. Overt authority used physical force; anonymous authority employs psychic manipulation." Fromm believes that the change from overt to anonymous authority was determined by the organizational needs of modern corporate society. In the modern industrial state the worker must become a cog that is managed and manipulated. Anonymous authority through bureaucratic procedures is the most effective means of control. The school by using anonymous authority prepares the individual for control by hidden bureaucratic authority. The worker is also prepared for the consumer market. Advertising as a persuasive form of coercion increases consumer appetites, creates new desires, and directs these desires into channels most profitable for industry. Fromm, like Ellul, believes that man becomes just a "thing" in the system and education is preparation to becoming a "thing." "Our economic system," he writes, "must create men who fit its needs; men who cooperate smoothly; men who want to consume more and more."[15]

It is interesting that educational critics, such as Erich Fromm, reject socialization in education for the very reasons that it was originally supported. Fromm abhors the idea of education producing men who are "willing to do what is expected of them, men who will fit into the social machine without friction, who can be led without leaders, and who can be directed without any aim except the one to 'make good.' "[16] These were, of course, the goals of social educators. In fact the American school system in the twentieth century was built upon these very same values. Fromm's negative reaction therefore is not toward an accidental development in education but toward a consciously sought-after goal that evolved with the industrial state.

The same is true of Jacques Ellul's criticism of the relationship between education and technology. For instance, Frank Parsons, the father of vocational guidance, would have applauded a system that matched and molded citizens for a job needed by the industrial system. Ellul finds this repulsive because man is treated like a technological "thing" and is not allowed to direct his life toward human needs. But treating humans like "things" was precisely what Parsons advocated. For him human happiness and technological efficiency were inseparable. For Ellul human happiness and technological efficiency are incompatible.

The real difference is in the model used to evaluate the world. Among the groups that have been considered at the beginning of the twentieth century, the model used was that of a machine-like corporate organization. Like the earlier members of the eighteenth century enlightenment many post–Civil War Americans have been enthralled with the idea of a clockwork universe. The industrial developments after the Civil War further impressed their minds with the potential value of a well-working machine. Social and economic problems organized into a machine model were reduced to problems of mechanical adjustment. It was found that the one limiting factor in making society work like a machine was the human being. Government and business companies could be organized into an efficient structure, but the organization was not functional unless human beings fulfilled their assigned roles. The ideal organization was that of a machine with specialized parts and coordinated activity. According to this model the health and happiness of any organization depended on smooth and efficient operation.

On a grand scale this model represented the well-working society as a series of interlocking corporate structures all humming away. Within the scheme the public schools became the central mechanism of social control feeding trained and conditioned workers and citizens into the whirring gears. Man as a natural resource was considered in the same terms as iron and timber. Education was to shape and mold raw humanity into the cooperative and specialized cog. This view of society was not the result of a conspiratorial plot. Immense social and economic problems did exist and there was need of some way to surmount them. This model was chosen because at the time it promised the best results. That education as social control meant limitation of freedom was immaterial to the needs of the social system. Humanitarian reformers made education a part of the corporate model because they believed that it would end poverty and industrial turmoil. Industrialists applied the model because they needed workers for their corporations and because it justified their own activities. The model promised to do good and make money at the same time.

By the middle of the century a certain pessimism developed about this type of social model because of a feeling that it was making money and not doing much good. Technology itself was dropped from its humanitarian pedestal when it was found that technology in war could destroy as well as build. The general feeling that runs through the writing of critics like Fromm and Ellul is that the model of human desires and needs must be imposed on the world and not vice versa.

Their attitude assumes that these can provide deeper satisfaction and meaning for each individual. It also assumes that there is something beyond the purely chemical and biological in man. The rejection of the idea that man can feel happiness to the full through conditioning and mechanical devices attached to nerve centers suggests that there is more satisfaction in self-conscious choice of ends and a struggle for their accomplishment. Being human, rather than a thing, would appear to mean experiencing life in its every dimension. Feeling happy is not enough. One must touch the low levels of despair and climb to the ecstasies of joy. Only through contact and living can one truly be human. These ideas do rest on the assumption that being human is in this sense worthwhile.

Faith in the traditional values of technology has continued through the twentieth century. By traditional is meant a non-McLuhanese concept of technology. Fromm's and Ellul's pessimism is not shared by the systems-analysis and computer-oriented educators. The new phenomenon is that of the computer's determining the model that will be used and that model's being applied to social organizations and individuals. This approach is considered good because like previous developments it is believed to promise a more efficient and productively rewarding system. The computer now provides the model because all data have to be arranged so that they can be handled by the computer mechanism. This is one of the revolutionary facts of the second industrial revolution. Because the computer is so rapid and efficient, all aspects of technology are made to fit it. This means that they have to be organized in certain limited ways to be utilized by the computer. Therefore to gain the benefits of the computer, the computer's pattern has to be used to organize experience. In other words, the functioning pattern of the computer provides the new organizational model.

The model borrowed from the computer, and one that horrifies Fromm and Ellul, is the systems analysis approach. This method, choosing from several models, organizes descriptive data into flow charts so that predictions and recommendations can be made from the original set of data. In a sense it is a streamlined form of scientific management. Applied to education it results in the same type of organization hoped for by previous educators. A predictive chart is constructed to show how the child can flow smoothly through the schools with his interests and aptitudes matched to appropriate courses that will lead to an appropriate job. On example of the application of systems technology to education is a project conducted by the Systems Development Corporation with a grant from the United States Office of Education. Five high schools were selected for intensive study. Flow diagrams of the schools were made to suggest new combinations of media and personnel to "accomplish the task of education more efficiently." One innovation was the surveillance and detection system, a system that would have delighted the early vocational guidance counselors. The computer center of the system would constantly receive data on the performance of each student. These data would include both academic test scores and teachers' reports on the student's interests, social and emotional conditions, and learning problems. The computer would survey these data and compare them with stored information concerning performance expectancies and past achievement. If the computer detected anything wrong, it would notify the appropriate personnel. The machine and model therefore would both diagnose and prescribe remedies. One of the leaders of the project states that the computer "would indicate the names of students who might need help, the kind of help that might be needed, and the names of the persons who should be alerted. Teachers, students, counselors, or administrative personnel might be alerted by the system."[17] The surveillance and detection system would create the clockwork world dreamed of in the enlightenment.

This approach does in fact turn man into a thing. The theory of human action which is most easily utilized in a systems method is behavioral psychology. Based on the theory that human actions are the result of stimulus-response conditioning and that all emotions are physically measurable, it provides a logical model that can be handled by the computer, probably the reason for the widespread popularity of the theory during the 1960's. The theory has resulted in lists of specific behavioral objectives which are used to determine the goals and the results of teaching. These lists reflect the idea that education should teach only those things that are measurable. The behavioral measurements can be easily used in a systems flow chart or in a computer. Behaviorists also define survival as the only innate goal for man. All other interests and desires are the result of related conditioning. This means that the behaviorist, in determining what specific behavior should be developed, has only survival as a criterion for deciding. Put in these terms, conditioning for the technological system is logical. As Ellul points out, it appears absolutely necessary because if the individual were not adapted to the system, social maladjustment and suffering might result.

Behavioral psychology also fits into the technological and automated system because it denies human freedom. Frazier, a main character in B. F. Skinner's utopian novel about a community based on behavioral engineering, tells his guests that freedom is only a feeling that results from doing what you have been conditioned to do. "We can achieve," he explains, "a sort of control under which the controlled, though they are following a code much more scrupulously than was ever the case under the old system, nevertheless feel free."[18] The basic assumption of behaviorism is that there is no human freedom for, if there were, scientific laws about behavior would be impossible. The belief that happiness and freedom are just feelings that can be manipulated is the most frightening part of the present direction of our technological society.

Socialization in the context of behavioral psychology plus systems analysis becomes a process of encouraging personalities that fit into the model. Like any institutional organization, certain behavioral patterns are required for its operation. A student showing an unwillingness to operate within this context, such as refusing to follow directions on programmed learning machines, would have to be viewed as a deviant. Indeed, since he would not be getting along in his environment, he would probably be showing all the psychological stresses of social maladjustment. For the further functioning of the educational system and the mental health of the student, social adaptation must take place. Man truly becomes a "thing" in this situation because the needs of the system determine the form of his behavior.

The combination of behavioral psychology and systems analysis also provides support for the traditional idea of education as social control. The denial of states of happiness or freedom as anything but feelings that are most easily achieved through manipulation of the personality confirms any predisposition on the part of educators to think that the good society will result from shaping human character. Skinner's utopian community, Walden Two, uses education as the essential form of control. Horace Mann probably would have been quite pleased with Skinner's ideas. For both, the ideal society would require only a few restrictive laws because everyone would be trained to be "good."

Even McLuhan's analysis of the present trend of technology results in a deterministic psychology. Man might be heading toward a global village but it is not through self-conscious actions. The driving forces, in McLuhan's terms, are the changes in technology. In fact, for McLuhan, man's history is nothing but the history of psychological and social changes caused by technological changes. Man truly does become a "thing." He organizes his experiences in a manner taught to him by his media and acts according to that organization.

Within the context of these present developments the continued use of concepts of socialization in the schools takes on a nightmarish quality. After all, the original purpose of social education at the turn of the century was to fit man into the industrial world. Education did turn men into things that had to be trained and molded for the requirements of society. Computers and automation are making these goals even more possible and inevitable. Even Dewey's original concern about creating a community has become irrelevant to modern conditions. This means, of course, that the sole function of socialization is now just social adaptation. The solution is not to change the goals and direction of socialization and social control. This is impossible. As long as the public schools take responsibility for the socialization of the child, social adaptation to the institution becomes inevitable. The standards of freedom and individual life styles are determined by the organizational requirements of the institutions. Any talk about changing the goals of socialization without considering these factors is meaningless. The only possible solution is ending the power of the school.

NOTES

CHAPTER ONE

1. Michael V. O'Shea, *Social Development and Education* (Cambridge, 1909), 272.

2. William Chandler Bagley, *The Educative Process* (New York, 1924), 62–64.

3. Charles N. Glaab and A. Theodore Brown, *A History of Urban America* (New York, 1967, 134–135.

4. L. S. Rowe, "Social Consequences of Cities," *Yale Review* (November 1901), 298–312.

5. Ray Stannard Baker, *American Chronicle* (New York, 1945), 1–146.

6. Jacob A. Riis, *How the Other Half Lives* (New York, 1890), 264.

7. Quoted in John A. Garraty's *Right-Hand Man: The Life of George Perkins* (New York, 1960), 301.

8. Samuel Gompers, *Seventy Years of Life and Labor* (New York, 1948), Vol. II, 19.

9. *Ibid.*, Vol. II, 110–112.

10. *Ibid.*, Vol. II, 20–22.

11. Garraty, 126–147.

12. *Ibid.*, 216–217.

13. George W. Perkins, *Modern Industrialism* (address given before the Southern Commercial Congress, Atlanta, Georgia, March 8, 1911), 2.

14. *Ibid.*, 8–11.

15. Gompers, Vol. II, 117.

16. Gordan Maurice Jensen, *The National Civic Federation: American Business in an Age of Social Change and Social Reform, 1900–1910* (Unpublished dissertation, Princeton University, 1956), 58–61.

17. See Marc Karson, *American Labor Unions and Politics* (Southern Illinois University Press, 1958), 126–137.

18. Jensen.

19. *Proceedings of the National Civic Federation* (1908), 10.

20. *Ibid.*, 19.

21. Garraty, 223.

22. "Second Annual Message," *The Works of Theodore Roosevelt, Memorial Edition* (New York, 1925), Vol. XVII, 164.

23. Garraty, 223.

24. "The New Nationalism," *The Works of . . . ,* Vol. XIX, 24.

25. See George E. Mowry's *Theodore Roosevelt and the Progressive Movement* (New York, 1960), 270–274.

26. "The Pioneer Spirit and American Problems," *The Works of . . . ,* 23.

27. "Address at the Semicentennial Celebration of the Founding of Agricultural Colleges in the United States, Lansing, Michigan, May 31, 1907," *The Works of . . . ,* Vol. XVIII, 172.

28. Eric F. Goldman, *Rendezvous with Destiny* (New York, 1962), 146–147.

29. Herbert Croly, *The Promise of American Life* (New York, 1964), 29.

30. *Ibid.*, 22.

31. *Ibid.*, 23.

32. *Ibid.*, 358–359.

33. *Ibid.*, 359.

34. *Ibid.*, 103.

35. *Ibid.*, 104.

36. *Ibid.*, 139.

37. *Ibid.*, 411.

38. *Ibid.*, 103.

39. *Ibid.*, 439.

40. *Ibid.*, 403.

41. *Ibid.*, 407.

42. *Ibid.*, 47.

43. Gabriel Kolko, *The Triumph of Conservatism* (Chicago, 1963), 217–279.

44. Kolko, 11–57, 279–307.

CHAPTER TWO

1. See E. Douglas Branch, *The Sentimental Years* (New York, 1965), 73–83.

2. William H. Tolman, *Social Engineering* (New York, 1909), 48.

3. E. Wake Cook, *Betterment: Individual, Social, and Industrial* (New York, 1906), 156.

4. *Ibid.*, 144.

5. Tolman, 32–37.

6. *Ibid.*, 48–60.

7. E. A. Filene, "The Social Improvement of Grammar School Graduates in Business Life," *Social Education Quarterly* (June 1907), 146–155.

8. Tolman, 132–182.

9. William H. Tolman, *Industrial Betterment* (New York, 1900), 9–11.

10. Edwin L. Shuey, *Factory People and Their Employers* (New York, 1900), 80–86; and Tolman, *Social Engineering*, 298–299.

11. Tolman, *Industrial Betterment*, 7–8.

12. Cook, 164–175, 220–222.

13. Tolman, *Industrial Betterment*, 10.

14. Tolman, *Social Engineering*, 318–319.

15. Stanley Buder, *Pullman—An Experiment in Industrial Order and Community Planning, 1880–1930* (New York, 1967), 140.

16. *Ibid.*, 36–37.

17. James B. Allen, *The Company Town in the American West* (Norman, Oklahoma, 1966), 57–69.

18. Tolman, *Social Engineering*, 38–41, 258–260.

19. Allen, 63.

20. See Samuel Haber's *Efficiency and Uplift—Scientific Management in the Progressive Era, 1890–1920* (Chicago, 1964), ix–x, 71.

21. Tolman, *Social Engineering*, 304.

22. *Ibid.*, 4.

23. Shuey, 52.

24. Tolman, *Social Engineering*, 61.

25. Filene, 149.

26. Tolman, *Social Engineering*, 28.

27. Shuey, 63.

28. Tolman, *Social Engineering*, 76.

29. *Ibid.*, 39.

30. *Ibid.*, 264.

31. *Examples of Welfare in the Cotton Industry* (undated), published by Committee on Welfare of the National Civic Federation, 1.

32. Tolman, *Social Engineering*, 303.

33. Buder, 62.

34. Tolman, *Social Engineering*, 286–289.

35. *Examples of Welfare . . .* , 7–8.

36. Tolman, *Social Engineering*, 264.

37. Tolman, *Industrial Betterment*, 38.

38. Tolman, *Social Engineering*, 258.

39. *Ibid.*, 265.

40. Tolman, *Industrial Betterment*, 30–31.

41. Shuey, 162–163.

42. Tolman, *Social Engineering*, 293–296; *Industrial Betterment*, 35–36; and Shuey, 101.

43. Tolman, *Social Engineering*, 43.

44. *Ibid.*, 275–276; and Filene, 149–154.

45. Tolman, *Social Engineering*, 261–262, 274; and Shuey, 103.

46. *Proceedings of the National Association of Manufacturers* (1897), p. 4.

47. *Ibid.* (1900), p. 153; (1903), p. 80; (1901), p. 124.

48. *Ibid.* (1905), 149–150.

49. *Ibid.* (1910), 3, 85.

50. *Proceedings of the American Federation of Labor* (1908), 234.

51. *Proceedings of the National Association of Manufacturers* (1911), 74.

52. See Lawrence A. Cremin's, *Transformation of the School* (New York, 1961), 50–57.

53. Bernice Fisher, *Industrial Education* (Madison, Wisconsin, 1967), 113–114.

CHAPTER THREE

1. Quoted in William O. Bourne's *History of the Public School Society of the City of New York* (New York, 1870), 18.

2. See J. Wickersham, *History of Education in Pennsylvania* (Lancaster, Pennsylvania, 1886), 284.

3. Quoted in George H. Martin, *The Evolution of the Massachusetts Public School System* (New York, 1923), 138.

4. *Report on Monitorial Instruction to the Boston School Committee; Boston, 1828*, reprinted in Ellwood Cubberley, *Readings in Public Education in the United States* (Cambridge, 1934), 137.

5. William Chandler Bagley, *Classroom Management* (New York, 1925), 32–35.

6. William Chandler Bagley, *The Educative Process* (New York, 1924), 62–64.

7. Bagley, *Classroom Management*, 18–40.

8. William Heard Kilpatrick, *The Project Method* (Teacher's College, 1918), 13.

9. John and Evelyn Dewey, *Schools of Tomorrow* (New York, 1962), 92.

10. Colin A. Scott, *Social Education* (Boston, 1908), 13.

11. Ira W. Howerth, "Education and the Social Ideal," *Educational Review* (September 1902), 163.

12. "The Social Motive in School Work," *The Francis W. Parker School Year Book* (June 1912), 7.

13. William McAndrew, "Social Education in High Schools," *Religious Education* (February 1913), 599.

14. Samuel T. Dutton, *Social Phases of Education in the School and the Home* (New York, 1899), 22.

15. John Dewey, "Teaching Ethics in the High School," *Educational Review* (November 1893), 316.

16. John Dewey, "Ethical Principles Underlying Education," *The Third Yearbook of the National Herbart Society* (Chicago, 1897), 31.

17. For a general description of the activities of the Dewey School see Katherine Camp Mayhew and Anna Camp Edwards, *The Dewey School: The Laboratory School of the University of Chicago 1896–1903* (New York, 1936), 39–271.

18. John Dewey, *The Child and the Curriculum—The School and Society* (Chicago, 1963), 9–12.

19. See Mayhew and Edwards.

20. Dewey, *School and Society*, 14.

21. *Ibid.*, 24.

22. John Dewey, "The School as Social Center," *Proceedings of the National Education Association* (1902), 381.

23. John Dewey, "My Pedagogic Creed," in *Dewey on Education*, edited by Martin Dworkin (Teachers College, 1959), 25.

24. Scott, 15.

25. *Ibid.*, 82–86.

26. "Social Education Association," leaflet included in bound volume of *Social Education Quarterly*, Vol. I.

27. Scott, 102–146.

28. *Ibid.*, 6.

29. *Ibid.*, 212.

30. *Ibid.*, 168–169.

31. Irving King, *Education for Social Efficiency* (New York, 1913), 232–251.

32. L. A. Clark, "Group-Work in the High Schools," *Elementary School Teacher* (February 1907), 335.

33. John A. Keith, "Socializing the Materials and Methods of Education," *Elementary School Teacher* (December 1907), 177.

34. Kilpatrick, 6.

35. *Ibid.,* 14.

36. William T. Whitney, *The Socialized Recitation* (New York, 1915), 23–26.

37. Charles L. Robbins, *The Socialized Recitation* (New York, 1920), 13.

38. Olivia Pound, "Social Reconstruction in the High School," *School and Society* (December 1921), 510.

CHAPTER FOUR

1. William S. Webb, "President General's Report," *Proceedings of the Second Annual Congress of the Sons of the American Revolution* (New York, 1891), 8.

2. T. J. Riley, "Increased Use of Public School Property," *American Journal of Sociology* (March 1906), 655–656.

3. Quoted in William O. Bourne's *History of the Public School Society of the City of New York* (New York, 1870), 17.

4. See Roy Lubove, *The Progressives and the Slums* (University of Pittsburgh, 1962), 28–31.

5. Jacob A. Riis, *A Ten Years' War* (Cambridge, 1900), 31.

6. Jacob A. Riis, *How the Other Half Lives* (New York, 1890), 33, 166–167, 185.

7. Riis, *A Ten Years' War,* 223.

8. Sadie American, "The Movement for Vacation Schools," *American Journal of Sociology* (November 1898), 310–312.

9. O. J. Milliken, "Chicago Vacation Schools," *American Journal of Sociology* (November 1898), 291–295.

10. Riis, *A Ten Years' War,* 221.

11. Milliken, 296.

12. Clarence E. Rainwater, *The Play Movement in the United States* (Chicago, 1922), 52.

13. Riis, *How the Other Half Lives,* 55.

14. Riis, *A Ten Years' War,* 202.

15. Sadie American, "The Movement for Small Play-grounds," *American Journal of Sociology* (September 1898), 167.

16. Joseph Lee, *Constructive and Preventive Philanthropy* (New York, 1906), 148–169.

17. American, "The Movement for Small Parks," 168.

18. Rainwater, 90–104.

19. Henry S. Curtis, *The Play Movement and Its Significance* (New York, 1917), 1–10.

20. Albert Shaw, "Vacation Camps and Boys' Republics," *Review of Reviews* (May 1896), 572.

21. Jacob Riis, *The Children of the Poor* (New York, 1892), 153–156.

22. Shaw, 572.

23. William R. George, *The Junior Republic* (New York, 1910), 6–7.

24. *Ibid.,* 2–237.

25. *Ibid.,* 84–85.

26. Riis, *Children of the Poor,* 215.

27. Lee, 190.

28. Riis, *Children of the Poor,* 296–297.

29. Clarence Arthur Perry, *Wider Use of the School Plant* (New York, 1910), 3–4.

30. Florence Milner, "School Management from the Side of Social Life," *School Review* (April 1899), 215–216.

31. H. T. Steeper, "Extra-Curricular Activities of the High School," *Education* (February 1919), 367.

32. Perry, 349–350.

33. Riis, *A Ten Years' War,* 185–189.

34. Perry, 154–158.

35. "Games and the Department of Education," *Our Country* (June 1898), 155–158.

36. Perry, 294–300.

37. *Ibid.,* 311.

38. *Ibid.,* 172–182.

39. *Ibid.,* 225–239.

40. Edward Ross, *Social Control: A Survey of the Foundations of Order* (New York, 1922), 164–177, 269, 422–433.

41. Quoted in George H. Martin's *The Evolution of the Massachusetts Public School System* (New York, 1894), 87–88.

42. *The Republic and the School* (Teachers College, 1957), edited by Lawrence A. Cremin, 98–101.

43. J. K. Paulding, "The Public School as a Centre of Community Life," *Educational Review* (February 1898), 148.

44. H. E. Scudder, "The Schoolhouse as a Centre," *Atlantic Monthly* (January 1896), 103–109.

45. John Dewey, "The School as Social Center," *National Education Association Proceedings* (1902), 373–383.

46. J. Stokes, "Public Schools as Social Centres," *Annual American Academy* (May 1904), 457–463.

47. G. R. Taylor, "City Neighbors at Play," *Survey* (July 2, 1910), 548–549.

48. "Social Center Work in Milwaukee," *Charity* (December 19, 1908), 441–442.

49. Clarence A. Perry, *The Social Centers of 1912–13* and *School Center Gazette 1919–1920* (Russell Sage Publications).

50. A. Gove, "Public Schoolhouses and Their Uses as Centers of Instruction and Recreation for the Community," *Education* (March 1897), 407–411.

51. Clarence A. Perry, *The School as a Factor in Neighborhood Development* (Russell Sage Foundation, 1914),

52. T. Bowlker, "Woman's Home-Making Function Applied to the Municipality," *American City* (Vol. VI, 1912), 863–869.

53. Edward J. Ward, "Little Red School House," *Survey* (August 7, 1909), 646–647.

54. Edward J. Ward, *The Social Center* (New York, 1913), 18.

55. William Howe Tolman, *Municipal Reform Movements in the United States* (New York, 1895).

56. Ray Stannard Baker, "Do It for Rochester," *The American Magazine* (September 1910), 683–696.

57. Ward, *The Social Center*, 175–183.

58. Baker, *op. cit.* See Charles N. Glaab and A. Theodore

Brown's *A History of Urban America* (New York, 1967),
212–219; and Samuel P. Hays, "The Politics of Reform in
Municipal Government in the Progressive Era," *Pacific
Northwest Quarterly* (October 1964), 157–161.

59. Tolman, 39.

60. Ward, *The Social Center*, 69.

61. Woodrow Wilson "The Need of Citizenship Organization," *American City* (October 1911), 265–269.

62. Perry, *op. cit.*, 3.

63. Clarence A. Perry, *The High School as a Social
Centre* (Russell Sage Foundation, 1914).

64. "Social Center—Center of Democracy," *Survey*
(September 1913), 675–677.

65. Samuel P. Hays, "The Politics of Reform in Municipal
Government in the Progressive Era," *Pacific Northwest
Quarterly* (October 1964), 157–161.

66. Hays, 163.

67. Sol Cohen, *Progressive and Urban School Reform*
(New York, 1964), 16–55.

68. H. E. Scudder, "The Schoolhouse as a Centre,"
Atlantic Monthly (January 1896), 106.

69. Quoted in Michael B. Katz's "The Emergence of
Bureaucracy in Urban Education: The Boston Case,
1860–1884," *The History of Education* (Quarterly, Vol. VII,
No. 3, Fall 1968), 349.

70. Katz, "The Emergence of Bureaucracy . . . ," Vol. VII,
No. 2 (Summer 1968) pp. 155–185, and Vol. VII, No. 3
(Fall 1968), 319–355.

71. Katz, Vol. VII, No. 2, 173–174.

CHAPTER FIVE

1. Frank Parsons, *Our Country's Need* (Boston, 1894), 69.

2. Hugo Munsterberg, *American Problems,* (New York,
1910), 27–28.

3. Eli W. Weaver, *Wage-Earning Occupations of Boys
and Girls* (Brooklyn, 1912).

4. J. Adams Puffer, *Vocational Guidance* (Chicago, 1913), 274.

5. Parsons, vi.

6. Frank Parsons, *The Drift of Our Time* (Chicago, 1898), 11.

7. Parsons, *Our Country's Need*.

8. Frederick G. Bonser, "Necessity of Professional Training for Vocational Counseling," *Vocational Guidance: Papers Presented at the Organization Meeting of the Vocational Association, Grand Rapids, Michigan, October 21–24, 1913* (United States Bureau of Education Bulletin, No. 14, 1914), 38.

9. Parsons, *Our Country's Need*, 2.

10. F. M. Giles, "Guidance by Systematic Courses of Instruction in Vocational Opportunities and Personal Characteristics," *Vocational Guidance: Papers Presented . . . , op. cit.*, 57–58.

11. Frank Parsons, *Choosing a Vocation* (Boston, 1909), 32–44.

12. Hugo Munsterberg, *Psychology and Industrial Efficiency* (Cambridge, 1913), 36–55.

13. Jesse B. Davis, *The Saga of a Schoolmaster* (Boston, 1956), 184–185.

14. Jesse B. Davis, *Vocational and Moral Guidance* (Boston, 1914), 46–123; and "Vocational and Moral Guidance in the High School," *Religious Education* (February 1913), 646.

15. Meyer Bloomfield, "Vocational Guidance in the High School," in Charles H. Johnston's *The Modern High School* (New York, 1914), 612.

16. *Ibid.*, 624.

17. Edward A. Krug, *The Shaping of the American High School* (New York, 1964), 330.

18. Quoted in the *Report of the Committee to Make a Survey of the Junior High Schools of the City of New York* (1924), 236.

19. Quoted in Krug, 328.

20. Quoted in *Report of the Committee . . .* , 119.

21. *Ibid.*, 118–119.

22. Philip Cox, "The Ben Blewett Junior High School: An Experiment in Democracy," *School Review* (May 1919), 345–359; and R. L. Lyman, "The Ben Blewett Junior High School," *School Review* (January 1920), 26–40.

23. Bloomfield, 610.

24. Edward L. Thorndike, "The Permanence of Interests and Their Relation to Abilities," in Meyer Bloomfield's *Readings in Vocational Guidance* (Boston, 1914), 386–395.

25. G. Stanley Hall, *Adolescence* (New York, 1904), Vol. I, XV.

26. G. Stanley Hall, "Childhood and Adolescence," in *Health, Growth, and Heredity*, eds. Charles E. Strickland and Charles Burgess (New York, 1965), 108.

27. Hall, *Adolescence*, Vol. II, 125.

28. *Ibid.*, Vol. II, 432.

29. Jane Addams, *The Spirit of Youth and the City Streets* (New York, 1909), 16.

30. *Ibid.*, 20.

31. *Ibid.*, 162.

32. Booth Tarkington, *Seventeen* (New York, 1915), 26.

33. *Ibid.*, 249.

34. "Tentative Report of the Committee on A System of Teaching Morals in the Public Schools," *National Education Association Proceedings (1911)*, 360.

35. *Ibid.*, 342–370.

36. Joseph Abelson, "A Study of the Junior High School Project," *Education* (September 1916), 11.

37. J. Adams Puffer, *The Boy and His Gang* (Boston, 1912), 38.

38. *Ibid.*, 41–153.

39. Cox, *op. cit.*

40. R. L. Lyman, "The Guidance Program of the Holmes Junior High School," *School Review* (February 1924), 93–104.

41. C. O. Davis, "Junior High Schools in the North Central Association Territory, 1917–18," *School Review* (May 1918), 335.

42. Cox, 346.

43. Thomas W. Gosling, "Educational Reconstruction in the Junior High School," *Educational Review* (May 1919), 384–385.

44. *Report of the Committee . . . , op. cit.,* 217.

45. *Ibid.,* 216.

46. N. C. Hieronimus, "The Teacher-Adviser in the Junior High School," *Educational Administration and Supervision* (February 1917), 91.

47. *Ibid.,* 92.

48. Helen Cowing, "The Four-Year Home-Room," *School and Society* (June 10, 1922), 627–629.

49. Emerson T. Cockrell, "The Home Room Period," *Junior High School Clearing House* (October 1923), 13.

50. R. L. Lyman, "The Washington Junior High School," *School Review* (March 1920), 178–204.

CHAPTER SIX

1. Quoted in Edward A. Krug, *The Shaping of the American High School* (New York, 1964), 320.

2. *Ibid.,* 397.

3. *Ibid.,* particularly chapters 11–15.

4. *Cardinal Principles of Secondary Education* (Bureau of Education, Bulletin 1918, 35).

5. For instance, Elbert K. Fretwell, "Extra-Curricular Activities of Secondary Schools," *Teachers College Record* (January 1923; January 1924; May 1926; June 1926; June 1927).

6. Thomas R. Briggs, "Extra-Curricular Activities in Junior High Schools," *Educational Administration and Supervision* (January 1922), 1–9.

7. William Bishop Owen, "Social Education Through the School," *School Review* (January 1907), 11–26.

8. *Cardinal Principles . . . ,* 20.

9. *Ibid.,* 20.

10. Wilson L. Gill, *A New Citizenship* (Hanover, Pennsylvania, 1913), 49.

11. Wilson Gill is listed as one of the twenty-one members of the first SAR convention and also as assistant-secretary. No mention is ever made of the author of the constitution. See John St. Paul, *The History of the National Society of the Sons of the American Revolution* (New Orleans, 1962), 12. I cannot find any mention of Wilson Gill in relation to the DAR. But inasmuch as the SAR was involved in its organization he probably was involved.

12. William S. Webb, *National Society of the Sons of the American Revolution* (New York, 1890), 7.

13. Chauncey M. Depew, "Oration of Chauncey M. Depew," *Proceedings of the Second Annual Congress of the Sons of the American Revolution* (New York, 1891), 64.

14. Wilson L. Gill, *Manual of the School Republic* (Madison, Wisconsin, 1932), 7.

15. "What Is the Matter with Americans Whose Brains Have Been Cultivated?" *Our Country* (October 1899), 1.

16. See Gill, *A New Citizenship*, 52; Bernard Cronson, *Pupil Self-Government* (New York, 1907), 3–5; and "A Summer Work of the Patriotic League," *Our Country* (September 1897), 1.

17. Delos F. Wilcox and Wilson F. Gill, "An Outline of American Government for Use in City and Country Schools in Connection with the Gill School City and Other Organizations for Self-Government," *Our Country* (October 1899), 3–109.

18. Alfred L. Beebe, "The Gill City Health Department," *Our Country* (June 1898), 177–186.

19. Gill, *A New Citizenship*, 198–204.

20. Albert Shaw, "The School City—A Method of Pupil Self-Government," *Review of Reviews* (December 1899), 673–686.

21. C. W. French, "School Government," *School Review* (January 1898), 35–44; and "The Problem of School Government," *School Review* (April 1900), 201–212.

22. Richard Welling, *As the Twig Is Bent* (New York, 1942).

23. *Ibid.*, 91.

Notes : : page 187

24. Reprinted in Richard Welling's *Self Government Miscellanies*.

25. William A. McAndrew, *School Review* (September 1897), 456–460.

26. Walter L. Phillips, "Pupil Co-operation in Self-Government," *Education* (April 1902), 543.

27. R. R. Smith, "Three Experiments in Pupil Self-Government," *Education* (December 1916), 230.

28. A. O. Bowden, "Student Self-Government," *School and Society* (July 27, 1918), 97.

29. Edward Rynearson, "Supervised Student Activities in the School Program," *First Yearbook, National Association of Secondary School Principals* (1917), 47–50.

30. D. E. Cloyd, "Student Organizations in City High Schools," *Education* (September 1910), 17–20.

31. Frank K. Phillips, "The School Paper," *Industrial Arts Magazine* (July 1917), 268–271. Reprinted in Joseph Roemer and Charles F. Allen's *Readings in Extra-Curricular Activities* (New York, 1929), 462–467.

32. Mary A. Sheehan, "Clubs—A Regular Social Activity," *The High School Journal* (October 1921), 132–135. Reprinted in Roemer and Allen, *ibid.*, 304.

33. V. K. Froula, "Extra-Curricular Activities: Their Relation to the Curricular Work of the School," *National Education Association Proceedings (1915)*, 738–39.

34. Harry P. Clarke and Willard Beatty, "Physical Training in the Junior High School," *The School Review* (Vol. 33, 1925), 532–540.

35. James Naismith, "High School Athletics and Gymnastics as an Expression of the Corporate Life of the High School," in Charles H. Johnston's, *The Modern High School* (New York, 1914), 440.

36. C. M. Howe, "The High-School Teacher and Athletics," *The School Review* (December 1923), 781–782.

37. "The Morning Exercise as a Socializing Influence," *Francis W. Parker School Year Book* (Chicago, 1913), 7–10.

38. *Ibid.*, 11.

39. *Ibid.*, 11.

40. Charles R. Foster, *Extra-Curricular Activities in the High School* (Richmond, Virginia, 1925), 108–109.

41. Eileen H. Galvin and M. Eugenia Walker, *Assemblies for Junior and Senior High Schools* (New York, 1929), 1.

42. Francis H. J. Paul, "The Growth of Character Through Participation in Extra-Curricular Activities," *The Fiftieth Yearbook of the Department of Secondary-School Principals* (1921), Vol. II, 54–60.

43. *Ibid.*

44. Burton P. Fowler, "Socialization of the Six-Year High School Through the Organization of Student Activities," *National Education Association Proceedings,* Vol. LIX, 672–673.

CHAPTER SEVEN

1. Upton Sinclair, *The Goose-Step: A Study of American Education* (Pasadena, California, 1922), p. 18.

2. George S. Counts, *The Social Composition of Boards of Education: A Study in the Social Control of Public Education* (Chicago, 1927), p. 87.

3. Lightner Witmer, *The Nearing Case* (New York, 1915), p. 3.

4. Scott Nearing, "Who's Who on Our Boards of Education," *School and Society* (January 20, 1917), Vol. V, No. 108, pp. 89–90.

5. Scott Nearing, "Who's Who Among College Trustees," *School and Society* (September 8, 1917), Vol. VI, No. 141, pp. 297–299.

6. Counts, p. 54.

7. *Ibid.*, pp. 82–85.

8. Sinclair, p. 91.

9. *Ibid.*, pp. 222–223.

10. *Ibid.*, pp. 181–182.

11. *Ibid.*, pp. 287–302.

12. Upton Sinclair, *The Goslings: A Study of the American Schools* (Pasadena, California, 1924), pp. 42–46.

13. *Ibid.*, pp. 72, 120–125, 144.

14. *Ibid.*, p. 276.

15. *Ibid.*, pp. 318–328, 268.

16. Joseph J. Cohen, "Stelton Was Young," in *The Modern School of Stelton* (Stelton, New Jersey, 1925), pp. 1–69.

17. *Ibid.*, p. 17.

18. Francisco Ferrer, "L'Ecole Renovee," *Mother Earth* (November 1909), Vol. IV, No. 9, pp. 267–275.

19. Harry Kelly, "The Modern School in Retrospect," in *The Modern School of Stelton, op cit.*, pp. 115–119.

20. James H. Dick, "Radicals and Education," *The Road to Freedom* (April 1929), Vol. V, No. 8, pp. 1–2.

21. Alexis C. Ferm, "Workers' Children and the Public Schools," *The Road to Freedom* (March 1931), Vol. 7, No. 7, p. 5.

22. Dick, p. 2.

23. Ferm, p. 5.

24. *Ibid.*, p. 5.

25. See Alexis C. Ferm, "A Biographical Note," in Elizabeth Byrne Ferm, *Freedom in Education* (New York, 1949), pp. 189–203.

26. See Elizabeth Burns Ferm, "Activity and Passivity of the Educator," *Mother Earth* (March 1907), Vol. II, No. 1, pp. 25–37.

27. Ernest H. Lindley, "The Universities and the People," *School and Society* (December 5, 1925), Vol. XXII, No. 571, pp. 697–702.

28. James H. Maurer, "Labor's Demand for Its Own Schools," *The Nation* (September 20, 1922), Vol. 115, No. 2985, pp. 276–278.

29. Devere Allen, "A School for Workers' Children," *The Nation* (October 15, 1924), Vol. 119, No. 3093, pp. 417–418.

30. "A New Community School," *Survey* (October 15, 1924), pp. 91–92.

31. Nellie M. Seeds, "Democracy in the Making at Manu-

mit School," *Nation* (June 1, 1927), Vol. 124, No. 3230, pp. 608–609.

32. *Ibid.*, p. 609.

33. Quoted in Counts, *op. cit.*, p. 86.

CHAPTER EIGHT

1. See James D. Koerner, *Who Controls American Education?* (Boston, 1968).

2. See Henry Allen Bullock's *A History of Negro Education in the South* (New York, 1970), pp. 60–147. I am also indebted to James Anderson for the opportunity to read his unpublished work on Booker T. Washington and his relationship to industrial leaders.

3. A. B. Hollingshead, *Elmstown's Youth* (New York, 1949).

4. Ivan Illich, *The Breakdown of Schools* (Cuernavaca, 1971).

5. Karl Marx, "Economic and Philosophical Manuscripts," in Erich Fromm's *Marx's Concept of Man* (New York, 1961), p. 98.

6. *Ibid.*, p. 103.

7. Marshall McLuhan, *Understanding Media: The Extensions of Man* (New York, 1966), p. 157.

8. *Ibid.*, p. 308.

9. *Ibid.*, p. 292.

10. See Henry Adams, *The Education of Henry Adams* (Cambridge, 1961), particularly chapters XXV–XXXV.

11. Jacques Ellul, *The Technological Society* (New York, 1967), 436.

12. *Ibid.*, p. 348.

13. *Ibid.*, p. 348.

14. *Ibid.*, pp. 359–360.

15. Erich Fromm's Foreword to A. S. Neill's *Summer-Hill* (New York, 1960).

16. *Ibid.*

Notes : : page 191

17. John F. Cogswell, "Systems Technology in Education," in *Man-Machine Systems in Education*, edited by John W. Loughary (New York, 1966), pp. 45–65.

18. B. F. Skinner, *Walden Two* (New York, 1948), p. 262.

BIBLIOGRAPHY

BOOKS

ADAMS, HENRY. *The Education of Henry Adams.* Boston, 1918.

ADDAMS, JANE. *The Spirit of Youth and the City Streets.* New York, 1909.

ALLEN, JAMES B. *The Company Town in the American West.* Norman, Oklahoma, 1966.

BAGLEY, WILLIAM CHANDLER. Classroom Management. New York, 1925.

————. *The Educative Process.* New York, 1924.

BAKER, RAY STANNARD. *American Chronicle.* New York, 1945.

BLOOMFIELD, MEYER. *Readings in Vocational Guidance.* Boston, 1915.

BOURNE, WILLIAM O. *History of the Public School Society of the City of New York.* New York, 1870.

BRANCH, E. DOUGLAS. *The Sentimental Years.* New York, 1934.

BUDER, STANLEY. *Pullman—An Experiment in Industrial Order and Community Planning, 1880–1930.* New York, 1967.

BULLOCK, HENRY ALLEN. *A History of Negro Education in the South.* New York, 1970.

Cardinal Principles of Secondary Education. Bureau of Education, Bulletin 1918, 35.

COHEN, JOSEPH J., AND ALEXIS C. FERM. *The Modern School of Stelton.* Stelton, N.J., 1925.

COHEN, SOL. *Progressive and Urban School Reform.* New York, 1964.

COOK, E. WAKE. *Betterment: Individual, Social, and Industrial.* New York, 1906.

CREMIN, LAWRENCE A. *Transformation of the School.* New York, 1961.

CROLY, HERBERT. *The Promise of American Life.* New York, 1909.

CRONSON, BERNARD. *Pupil Self-Government.* New York, 1907.

COUNTS, GEORGE. *The Social Composition of Boards of Education: A Study in the Social Control of Public Education.* Chicago, 1927.

CURTIS, HENRY S. *The Play Movement and Its Significance.* New York, 1917.

DAVIS, JESSE B. *The Saga of a Schoolmaster.* Boston, 1956.

————. *Vocational and Moral Guidance.* Boston, 1914.

DEWEY, JOHN. *The Child and the Curriculum—The School and Society.* Chicago, 1963.

DEWEY, JOHN AND EVELYN. *Schools of Tomorrow.* New York, 1915.

Dewey on Education. Martin Dworkin, editor. New York, 1959.

DUTTON, SAMUEL T. *Social Phases of Education in the School and the Home.* New York, 1899.

ELLUL, JACQUES. *The Technological Society.* New York, 1967.

Examples of Welfare in the Cotton Industry. Published by the Committee on Welfare of the National Civil Federation, Undated.

FERM, ELIZABETH. "Activity and Passivity of the Educator," *Mother Earth* (March 1907), Vol. II, No. 1.

FOSTER, CHARLES R. *Extra-Curricular Activities in the High School.* Richmond, Virginia, 1925.

The Francis W. Parker School Yearbook. Chicago, 1912 and 1913.

FROMM, ERICH. Foreword to A. S. Neill's *Summerhill.* New York, 1960.

————. *Marx's Concept of Man.* New York, 1961.

GALVIN, EILEEN H., AND EUGENIA M. WALKER. *Assemblies for Junior and Senior High Schools.* New York, 1929.

GARRATY, JOHN A. *Right-Hand Man: The Life of George Perkins.* New York, 1960.

GEORGE, WILLIAM R. *The Junior Republic.* New York, 1910.

GILL, WILSON L. *A New Citizenship.* Hanover, Pennsylvania, 1913.

————. *Manual of the School Republic.* Madison, Wisconsin, 1932.

GINGER, RAY. *Altgeld's America.* New York, 1958.

GLAAB, CHARLES N., AND A. THEODORE BROWN. *A History of Urban America.* New York, 1967.

GOLDMAN, ERIC F. *Rendezvous with Destiny.* New York, 1952.

GOMPERS, SAMUEL. *Seventy Years of Life and Labor.* New York, 1948.

HABER, SAMUEL. *Efficiency and Uplift: Scientific Management in the Progressive Era 1890–1920.* Chicago, 1964.

HALL, G. STANLEY. *Adolescence.* New York, 1904.

Health, Growth, and Heredity. Edited by Charles E. Strickland and Charles Burgess. New York, 1965.

HOLLINGSHEAD, A. B. *Elmstown's Youth.* New York, 1949.

JENSEN, GORDON MAURICE. *The National Civic Federation: American Business in an Age of Social Change and Social Reform, 1900–1910.* Unpublished dissertation, Princeton University, 1956.

JOHNSTON, CHARLES R. *The Modern High School.* New York, 1914.

KARSON, MARC. *American Labor Unions and Politics.* Southern Illinois University Press, 1958.

KILPATRICK, WILLIAM HEARD. *The Project Method.* New York, 1918.

KING, IRVING. *Education for Social Efficiency.* New York, 1913.

KOLKO, GABRIEL. *The Triumph of Conservatism.* Chicago, 1963.

KRUG, EDWARD A. *The Shaping of the American High School.* New York, 1964.

LEE, JOSEPH. *Constructive and Preventive Philanthropy.* New York, 1906.

LUBOVE, ROY. *The Progressives and the Slums.* Pittsburgh, 1962.

MC LUHAN, MARSHALL. *Understanding Media: The Extensions of Man.* New York, 1966.

Man-Machine Systems in Education. Edited by John W. Loughary. New York, 1966.

MARTIN, GEORGE H. *The Evolution of the Massachusetts Public School System.* New York, 1894.

MAYHEW, KATHERINE CAMP, AND ANNA CAMP EDWARDS. *The Dewey School: The Laboratory School of the University of Chicago 1896–1903.* New York, 1936.

MOWRY, GEORGE E. *Theodore Roosevelt and the Progressive Movement.* New York, 1960.

MUNSTERBERG, HUGO. *American Problems.* New York, 1910.

_____. *Psychology and Industrial Efficiency.* Cambridge, 1913.

O'SHEA, MICHAEL. *Social Development and Education.* Cambridge, 1909.

PARSONS, FRANK. *Choosing a Vocation.* Boston, 1909.

_____. *The Drift of Our Time.* Chicago, 1898.

_____. *Our Country's Need.* Boston, 1894.

PERKINS, GEORGE W. *Modern Industrialism.* Atlanta, Georgia, 1911.

PERRY, CLARENCE A. *The High School as a Social Centre.* Russell Sage Foundation, 1914.

_____. *The School as a Factor in Neighborhood Development.* Russell Sage Foundation, 1914.

_____. *School Center Gazette 1919–1920.* Russell Sage Publications.

_____. *The Social Centers of 1912–1913.* Russell Sage Publications.

_____. *Wider Use of the School Plant.* New York, 1910.

PUFFER, J. ADAMS. *The Boy and His Gang.* Boston, 1912.

_____. *Vocational Guidance.* Chicago, 1913.

RAINWATER, CLARENCE E. *The Play Movement in the United States.* Chicago, 1922.

Readings in Extra-Curricular Activities. Edited by Joseph Roemer and Charles F. Allen. New York, 1929.

The Republic and the School. Edited by Lawrence A. Cremin. New York, 1957.

RIIS, JACOB. *A Ten Years' War.* Cambridge, 1900.

_____. *How the Other Half Lives.* New York, 1890.

_____. *The Children of the Poor.* New York, 1892.

ROBBINS, CHARLES L. *The Socialized Recitation.* New York, 1920.

ROOSEVELT, THEODORE. *The Works of Theodore Roosevelt, Memorial Edition.*

ROSS, EDWARD. *Social Control: A Survey of the Foundations of Order.* New York, 1922.

ST. PAUL, JOHN. *The History of the National Society of the Sons of the American Revolution.* New Orleans, 1962.

SCOTT, COLIN A. *Social Education.* Boston, 1908.

SHUEY, EDWIN L. *Factory People and Their Employers.* New York, 1900.

SINCLAIR, UPTON. *The Goose-Step: A Study of American Education.* Pasadena, California, 1922.

_____. *The Goslings: A Study of the American Schools.* Pasadena, California, 1924.

SKINNER, B. F. *Walden Two.* New York, 1948.

TARBELL, IDA M. *New Ideals in Business.* New York, 1916.

TARKINGTON, BOOTH. *Seventeen.* New York, 1915.

The Third Yearbook of the National Herbart Society. Chicago, 1897.

TOLMAN, WILLIAM H. *Industrial Betterment.* New York, 1900.

_____. *Municipal Reform Movements in the United States.* New York, 1895.

_____. *Social Engineering.* New York, 1909.

WARD, EDWARD J. *The Social Center.* New York, 1913.

WEAVER, ELI W. *Wage-Earning Occupations of Boys and Girls.* Brooklyn, 1912.

WEBB, WILLIAM S. *National Society of the Sons of the American Revolution.* New York, 1890.

WELLING, RICHARD. *As the Twig is Bent.* New York, 1942.

_____. *Self-Government Miscellanies.* (Undated.)

WHITNEY, WILLIAM T. *The Socialized Recitation.* New York, 1915.

WITMER, LIGHTNER. *The Nearing Case.* New York, 1915.

WICKERSHAM, J. *History of Education in Pennsylvania.* Lancaster, Pennsylvania, 1886.

PERIODICALS

American City.
American Journal of Sociology.
The American Magazine.
Annual American Academy.
Atlantic Monthly.
Education.
Educational Administration and Supervision.
Educational Review.
Elementary School Teacher.
Junior High School Clearing House.
Modern School.
Mother Earth.
Nation.
Our Country.
Religious Education.
Review of Reviews.
Road to Freedom.
School and Society.
School Review.
Social Education Quarterly.
Survey.
Teachers College Record.
Yale Review.

PROCEEDINGS

American Federation of Labor.
National Association of Manufacturers.
National Civic Federation.
National Education Association.
Sons of the American Revolution.
Vocational Guidance: Papers Presented at the Organization Meeting of the Vocational Association. Grand Rapids, Michigan. October 21–24, 1913. United States Bureau of Education, Bulletin No. 14, 1914.

INDEX